(UN)WILLING COLLECTIVES

TRANSMISSION

Transmission denotes the transfer of information, objects or forces from one place to another, from one person to another. Transmission implies urgency, even emergency: a line humming, an alarm sounding, a messenger bearing news. Through Transmission interventions are supported, and opinions overturned. Transmission republishes classic works in philosophy, as it publishes works that re-examine classical philosophical thought. Transmission is the name for what takes place.

(UN)WILLING COLLECTIVES:
ON CASTORIADIS, PHILOSOPHY AND POLITICS

Toula Nicolacopoulos and George Vassilacopoulos

re.press Melbourne 2018

re.press

http://www.re-press.org

© T. Nicolacopoulos & G. Vassilacopoulos 2018
The moral rights of the authors have been asserted

National Library of Australia Cataloguing-in-Publication entry

Nicolacopoulos, Toula, author.

(Un)Willing Collectives
Toula Nicolacopoulos and George Vassilacopoulos.

ISBN: 9780992373450 (paperback)

Series: Transmission.

Cover image: George Michelakakis, Magazines, 1995
Cover design and typesetting: Frixos Ioannides

Other Authors/Contributors: Vassilacopoulos, George, author.

CONTENTS

To Kosta for always challenging authorities

ACKNOWLEDGEMENTS

We, the authors, thank the publishers of the following journals for permission to include in the present work parts of some of our earlier articles:

'Cave Dwellers or Labyrinth Diggers? Castoriadis and Plato on Philosophy and Politics', *Critical Horizons*, vol. 18, 2017, pp. 119-135.

'The Time of Radical Autonomous Thinking and Social-historical Becoming in Castoriadis', *Thesis Eleven*, vol. 120, no. 1, 2014, pp. 59-74.

'"What ought we to think?": Castoriadis' Response to the Question for Thinking', *Cosmos and History: The Journal of Natural and Social Philosophy*, vol. 8, no. 2, 2012, pp. 21-33.

'George Michelakakis: Art as Recollecting Goya's The Third of May', *Journal of Modern Greek Studies (Australia and New Zealand)*, vol. 19, 2018, pp. 209-226.

An earlier version of Chapter 4 appeared under the title 'Radical Democratic Subjectivity: Possibilities and Limits' in Vrasidas Karalis (ed.), *Cornelius Castoriadis and Radical Democracy*, vol. 16, Leiden and Boston, Brill, 2014, pp. 262-290.

1. INTRODUCTION:
ELEMENTS OF A CRITIQUE

The focus of this study is on Castoriadis's intellectual practice. Broadly speaking Castoriadis's thought belongs to the libertarian communist tradition.[1] While his contribution as a critic of capitalism and thinker of socialist revolution has been the subject of discussion,[2] less attention has been paid to Castoriadis as a *revolutionary thinker*, as distinct from a thinker and practitioner *of the revolution*. We will be addressing the question 'what are the connections between Castoriadis's aspirations as a socialist intellectual and as a

1. See Chamsy Ojeili, 'Post-Marxism with Substance', *New Political Science*, vol. 23, no. 2, 2001, pp. 225-239 at p. 229.

2. See for example, Angelos T. Vouldis, 'Cornelius Castoriadis on the Scope and Content of Neoclassical and Marxian Economics', *Journal of Economic Issues*, vol. 52, no. 3, 2018; Vangelis Papadimitropoulos, 'Rational Mastery in the Work of Cornelius Castoriadis', *Capitalism Nature Socialism*, vol. 29, no. 3, 2018; Giorgio Baruchello, 'Old Bedfellows: Cornelius Castoriadis on Capitalism and Freedom', in Ingrid S. Straume and Giorgio Baruchello (eds.), *Creation Rationality and Autonomy: Essays on Cornelius Castoriadis*, Copenhagen, Denmark, Aarhus University Press NSU, 2013, pp. 101-129; Karl E. Smith, 'The Constitution of Modernity: A Critique of Castoriadis', *European Journal of Social Theory*, vol. 12, no. 4, pp. 505-521; Takis Fotopoulos, 'The Autonomy Project and Inclusive Democracy: A Critical Review of Castoriadis' Thought', *The International Journal of Inclusive Democracy*, vol. 4, no. 2. 2008, pp. 1-13; and Yorgos Oikonomou, 'Plato and Castoriadis: The Concealment and the Unravelling of Democracy', *The International Journal of Inclusive Democracy*, vol. 2, no. 1. 2005, pp. 1-15. See also Axel Honneth, 'Rescuing the Revolution with an Ontology: On Cornelius Castoriadis' Theory of Society', *Thesis Eleven*, no. 14, 1986, pp. 62-78.

philosopher of politics?' For Castoriadis, intellectuals are broadly those who 'irrespective of their profession, try to go beyond their sphere of specialization and actively inter-est themselves in what is going on in society'; they there-fore embody 'the very definition of the democratic citizen'.[3] Without rejecting the need for socialists' organizations,[4] Castoriadis prioritizes the genuinely egalitarian spirit of democratic citizenship:

> To be revolutionary signifies both to think that only the masses in struggle can resolve the problems of social-ism and not to fold one's arms for all that; it means to think that the essential content of the revolution will be given by the masses' creative, original and unforesee-able activity, and to act oneself, beginning with a ratio-nal analysis of the present and with a perspective that anticipates the future.[5]

Castoriadis analyses present conditions through elucida-tion, the work of digging down and exploring phenomena in their multiple and diverse modes, rather than by enlisting pre-determined concepts through which to make sense of the world.[6] This world is currently the field of global capital-ism and its institution of the time of accumulation, rational mastery and the static repetition of the same. Ultimately it is neo-liberal privatized subjectivity—the subject in their ca-pacity as the private person engaging in capitalist exchange relations—that Castoriadis confronts (in himself and his

---

3. Cornelius Castoriadis, *Philosophy Politics Autonomy: Essays in Political Philosophy*, David Ames Curtis (ed.), New York and Oxford, Oxford University Press, 1991, p. 5.

4. See for example, Christophe Premat's discussion of Castoriadis's views on workers Councils: Chirstophe Premat, 'Castoriadis and the Modern Political Imaginary—Oligarchy, Representation, Democracy', *Critical Horizons*, vol. 7, no. 1., pp. 251-275 at p. 268. On deliberative mechanisms of decision making see also Andreas Kalyvas, 'The Politics of Autonomy and the Challenge of Deliberation: Castoriadis contra Habermas', *Thesis Eleven*, vol. 64, no. 1, 2001, pp. 1-19 at p. 10.

5. Cornelius Castoriadis, *Political and Social Writings, Vol. I 1946-55*, Minneapolis, University of Minnesota Press, 1988, p. 298.

6. See Joel Whitebook, 'Review of Crossroads in the labyrinth', *Telos*, vol. 63, 1985, p. 23.

reader) and whose radical imagination he seeks to awaken and move towards the revolutionary practices of an autonomous collective consisting of those who are knowingly engaged in willing the radical transformation of society. While social transformation is generally a matter of social doing as the work of the masses, the conditions of modernity have given rise to subjectivation processes that make possible autonomous thought and action capable of exposing and disrupting heteronomous society. Accordingly, Castoriadis's political project of autonomy draws on the alignment of the masses (the anonymous collective) with society's self-instituting power (radical imaginary creativity) in relation to the laws and institutions of society (the instituted). The thinker of autonomy thinks by situating himself in the horizon of this project.

We will examine Castoriadis's elucidation of autonomous being and thinking, both in relation to the demands of his account of the political project of autonomy and by way of the contrast he draws with the inherited intellectual tradition, notably Plato and Hegel. This is a tradition Castoriadis takes to reinforce the prevalence of heteronomy throughout the social-political history of the West and thus to work against instituting genuine democracy. Our approach will be to juxtapose Castoriadis's reading of the history of the Greco-western world in terms of 'the struggle between autonomy and heteronomy'[7] with an alternative picture that emerges if we follow Hegel's diagnosis of modernity's ontological and conceptual limits and, in particular, his ascription of a decisive formative role to modern radically individualized proprietary being. Against the background of our Hegelian view, the question arises whether Castoriadis's idea of radical democratic subjectivity and his corresponding intellectual practice inadvertently conform to the character of the Hegelian 'empty' self that underpins property-owning subjectivity and, hence, to a mode of being that

---

7. Cornelius Castoriadis, 'The Greek Πόλις and the Creation of Democracy' in R. Lily, (ed.), *The Ancients and the Moderns*, Bloomington, Indiana, Indiana University Press, 1996, pp. 29-58 at p. 33.

can do no more than protest against its emptiness instead of offering genuine alternatives that take thinking beyond the choices available to it by the dominant orientation of formalism. For Castoriadis, of course, Hegel's account of history in terms of the unfolding of absolute spirit illustrates the problematic tendency of western inherited thought to deny the ontology of creation and hence to reinforce the prevalence of heteronomy. From his perspective the heteronomy of inherited thought stems from its reduction of being and temporality to determinacy and spatiality. Even Hegel, who is recognized as having 'transformed metaphysics from a spatial to a temporal construction',[8] does so, according to Castoriadis, only by reducing the temporal to a variation of the spatial.[9] Here we leave to one side this broader interpretive issue in order to test Castoriadis's understanding of radical democratic subjectivity and autonomous thinking against the background of the Hegelian account of modernity's limits.

Our overall aim will be to argue that Castoriadis inadvertently enacts the formal closure of the power of instituting he assigns to the autonomous collective. We demonstrate this claim by examining the way in which the idea of autonomy as enacted in Castoriadis' own intellectual practice is based on axiomatic decisions that privilege: (1) willing over receiving; and (2) signification over significance.[10] While the idea of *receiving significance* will be shown to operate implicitly in Castoriadis' critique of contemporary modes of heteronomous subjectivity, *receiving significance as part of the enacting of autonomy* will be shown to be Castoriadis's

8. Agnes Heller, 'Philosophy as Literary Genre', *Thesis Eleven*, vol. 10, no. 1, pp. 17-26 at p. 20.

9. Cornelius Castoriadis, *The Imaginary Institution*, pp.189-190.

10. 'Significance' does not name a psychic power of humans as, for example, the power of cathexis understood as 'the capacity to assign value to social imaginary significations' that are 'determined as such—as objects—by the instituted social-historical domain': Gerasimos Karavitis, 'On the Concept of Politics: A Comparative Reading of Castoriadis and Badiou', *Constellations*, vol. 25, 2018, pp. 256-271 p. 258. For whereas the redirection of cathexis may result in a new signification, significance or, more precicely, its being received is the presupposition of the exercise of such a power.

blind spot. This idea of significance stems from the historical appearance of the collective which, in the simplicity of its gathering communality, is at once complete and incomplete, stasis and movement, place and time. It is complete as a potentially universal power of affirming the singular being of individuals who, in receiving this power, are posited as gathered. It is incomplete in so far as such receiving also becomes the vision of gathering the collective through creation of forms (significations) out of its formlessness. This is what we call 'the (un)willing collective'. In European modernity (un)willing collectives appear with the French Revolution, activating the being of communal significance. Here we introduce these ideas by way of a brief interpretation of David's *The Tennis Court Oath*.

This artwork depicts a multiplicity of singular beings gathered and rendered as significant in the communal gathering, while the collective shows itself to be the fundamental orientation of humanity. As the raising of the embracing arms of the centred gathering figure suggest, 'to be' means to be as a gathered-gatherer of everyone in the infinitely embracing gathering of a self-conscious history that nonetheless looks toward the future. Whereas the gathering locates its universal orientation of togetherness in the singularity of singular being, the singular being of every individual encounters its own orientation as a gatherer in the communal spaces of the gathering *as already gathered*. In his *Phenomenology of Spirit* Hegel describes the simplicity of this mode of formless communal being as the 'undivided Substance of absolute freedom' in which 'all social groups or classes which are the spiritual spheres into which the whole is articulated are abolished'.[11] The revolutionary negation in question enacts a limitless gathering, which operates as the place from which the infinite task of freely re-gathering itself through the visionary willing of gathered yet diverse singular beings is announced as a project. The command of the collective is 'gather as already gathered'.

---

11. G.W.F. Hegel, *The Phenomenology of Spirit*, Oxford, Oxford University Press, 1970. #585.

At the same time, in depicting the gathered members of the communal space as enactors of the gathering, *The Tennis Court Oath* also signifies the subjective interiority of the externalized communal gathering. This is where the multiple differently preoccupied individual faces of David's figures acquire their supreme significance. The manifestation of the face in its irreplaceable uniqueness signifies the willing presence of the singular self in the public communal space. As the site of the intense concentration of the individual body as (participant in) the constitution of the whole, David's faces, consumed by their visionary circular gathering(s), not only signify the internalized communal gathering, they are also the source of the 'we'. Silencing time in the form of a visual articulation of the gathering's origin, *The Tennis Court Oath* elevates itself to a spatial instance in which the gathering is gathered and in doing so also elevates its creator to the gatherer who gathers the collective as the bearer of the principle, or orientation, of communality. In this visual articulation of the 'we', the artwork and the artist can be read as radically affirming the communal gathering as their ultimate source of meaning and significance.

Castoriadis rejects any discourse that places the being of the social, whether as society or as the speaking subject, in 'an intemporal always' in the name of society's historicity.[12] Whether or not and how he might nonetheless situate himself in a similar relationship to the dynamic of the (un)willing collective remains to be seen.

We begin our study of Castoriadis's intellectual practice in Chapter 2 by first outlining key aspects of his social and political ontology. After introducing the idea of time as creation and creativity, we highlight the differences between Castoriadis's notion of radical democracy and democratic subjectivity in comparison to the currently dominant consumerist conceptions that are rightfully the subject of critique. Then in Chapter 3 we draw out the implications of this theory for the labour of *autonomous* thinking. The notions of radical imaginary time, democratic politics and

---

12. Cornelius Castoriadis, *The Imaginary Institution*, p. 214–215.

autonomous thinking lead us to view the thinking of autonomy as a visionary practice and so to the question, 'how does
the visionary thinker understood as the champion of radical
autonomy activate this visionary practice?' Through an examination of the claim that the orientation of autonomy depends upon its being activated by a willing singularity who
accepts the Chaos of society and of the world, we argue that
Castoriadis's position presupposes an effective contrast between the autonomy of significance that he advocates and
the heteronomy of insignificance that he laments.

In Chapter 4 we draw upon Castoriadis's discussion of
the difference between autonomous and heteronomous responses to the Chaos to explain how he might distinguish
radical democratic subjectivity from pseudo-democrats.
Then drawing on Hegel's account of the development of subjectivity in the modern world we argue that Castoriadis's reliance on the will to accept the Chaos fails to distinguish radical democratic subjectivity because the generalized practice
of owning that cuts across consumerist and radical democratic activities in capitalist society, also exposes the Chaos
of the world. Having concluded that Castoriadis thus fails to
demonstrate the possibility of radical democratic practice in
the current reality, we then locate the conceptual source of
this failure in Castoriadis's way of privileging the power of
instituting and questioning. In the same chapter we will explain how Castoriadis's conceptual framework gives priority
to the power of instituting and show how this inadvertently
commits Castoriadis's conception of radical democratic subjectivity to the empty formalism that Hegel relates to modern proprietary being.

In Chapter 5 we contrast our reading of Plato's story of
the cave to show how Castoriadis's overestimation of the
power of questioning and of creating new social forms leads
him to overlook the importance of receiving significance. We
then proceed to argue that Castoriadis and Plato emerge as
two extremes. Whereas the first favours the power of questioning to the exclusion of receiving, the second privileges
the power of receiving over creation and creativity. Having

identified the inability of Castoriadis's mode of philosophical thinking to illuminate an implicit notion of receiving significance, in Chapter 6 we complete our investigation of his intellectual practice through analysis of the limits of his formulation of philosophy's fundamental question, 'what ought we to think?'.

2. AUTONOMOUS THINKING AND RADICAL IMAGINARY TIME

> We cannot think of time if we do not rid ourselves of a certain way—the inherited way—of thinking of being, that is to say, of positing being as determinacy. [...] It is fatal to the inherited referential thinking that there is no real *place* for time or that time cannot really *take place* (= exist) precisely because we must look for a place for time, an ontologically determined place in the determinacy of what is, hence that time is but a mode of place.[13]

For Castoriadis, inherited thought unavoidably reduces being to determinacy and consequently can do no more than (mis)treat time as *secondary* to such being.[14] The challenge is to think the being/becoming of time in its own terms but to do so is to allow for that which 'identitary thinking' is incapable of, namely time's 'essential indetermination' that, as Jeff Klooger argues, is 'a ferment which gives rise to creation itself'.[15] To take seriously time's existence—its taking

---

13. Cornelius Castoriadis, *The Imaginary Institution*, p. 191.

14. For a reading of Castoriadis's understanding of time as otherness in connection with Aristotle's use of number in his definition of time see Kristina Egumenovska, 'The Wreath of Subjectivity and Time', in Ingrid S. Straume and Giorgio Baruchello (eds.), *Creation Rationality and Autonomy: Essays on Cornelius Castoriadis*, Copenhagen, Denmark, Aarhus University Press NSU, 2013, pp. 229-241.

15. Cornelius Castoriadis, *World in Fragments: Writings on Politics, Society, Psychoanalysis and the Imagination*, California, Stanford

place ontologically—in an essentially indeterminate world is to appreciate that 'the world—being—is essentially 'Chaos, Abyss, Groundlessness'.[16] Being and time ultimately share the same characteristics: 'the unfolding of otherness, the deployment of alterity together with a dimension of identity/difference'.[17] This is why 'the fullness of being is given—that is, simply is—only in and through the emergence of otherness which is solidary with time'.[18] What the inherited tradition fails to realize then is that 'time is the excess of being over itself, that by which being is always essentially to be'.[19]

> Time can exist only if there is an emergence of what is other, of what is in no way *given with* what is, what does not *go together* with it. Time is the emergence of *other* figures. [...] It is the otherness—alteration of figures and, originally and in its core, it is this alone. These figures are other, not depending on what they *are not* (their place *in time*) but depending on *what* they *are*, they are inasmuch as they shatter determinacy, inasmuch as they cannot themselves be determined, on the basis of determinations that are 'external' to them.[20]

For social being, by which Castoriadis includes both society

University Press, 1997, p. 31; *The Imaginary Institution*, pp. 199–200. Jeff Klooger, *Castoriadis: Psyche, Society, Autonomy*, Leiden and Boston, Brill, 2009, p. 98. Jodi Heap, *The Imagination: The Seed of Indeterminacy in the Writings of Kant, Fichte and Castoriadis*, PhD dissertation, University of Melbourne, 2017. On the relationship of indeterminacy to creation see see also Vangelis Papadimitropoulos, 'Indeterminacy and creation in the work of Cornelius Castoriadis', *Cosmos and History: Journal of Natural and Social Philosophy*, vol. 11, no. 1, 2015, pp. 256-268.

16. Cornelius Castoriadis, *World in Fragments*, p.314. For an extensive discussion of Castoriadis's notion of indeterminacy see Jeff Klooger, *Castoriadis*, pp. 213-70; Jeff Klooger, 'The Guise of Nothing: Castoriadis on Indeterminacy, and its Misrecognition in Heidegger and Sartre', *Critical Horizons* vol. 14, no. 1, 2013, pp. 1-21. For an introduction to the early influences on Castoriadis's formation of these ideas see Vrasidas Karalis, 'Introduction to Cornelius Castoriadis's Early Essays', in Vrasidas Karalis (ed.), *Cornelius Castoriadis and Radical Democracy*, Leiden and Boston, Brill, 2014, pp. 1-20.

17. Cornelius Castoriadis, *World in Fragments*, p. 400.

18. Cornelius Castoriadis, *World in Fragments*, p. 401.

19. Cornelius Castoriadis, *World in Fragments*, p. 322.

20. Cornelius Castoriadis, *The Imaginary Institution*, p. 193.

and the psychic subject, time takes place at the fundamental ontological level—the level of the existence of social beings in general and not just of the phenomenological experience of psychic subjects—with the emergence of the radically new or, in other words, it is creation, which is itself being/ to be.[21] The other figures with whose emergence the time of creation comes into existence are distinguishable in that they are not externally determined; radical alterity contrasts with the merely different that is derivable from elsewhere.[22] In the movement from a figure's non-being to its being, time 'as otherness-alteration' not only 'comes from nothing and out of nowhere'[23] but also *brings itself* into being as new or as other and not simply as a consequence or as a different exemplar of the same'.[24] As Stathis Gourgouris explains, since this 'nothing' out of which radical creation emerges exists, in the most precise sense, *in* the world',

> we [modern humans] have to allow ourselves the paradoxical capacity to imagine both that this nothing, this non-being, is worldly, and that, instantly on coming to be something this newly created being registers its worldliness by an unavoidable encounter with what exists.[25]

21. For a discussion of the benefits to anti-foundationalism of Castoriadis's approach by comparison with Foucault's strategy of avoiding ontology see Alexandros Kioupkiolis, 'The Agonistic Turn of Critical Reason: Critique and Freedom in Foucault and Castoriadis', *European Journal of Social Theory*, vol. 15, no. 3, 2012, pp. 385-402 at pp. 388-393.

22. Cornelius Castoriadis, *The Imaginary Institution*, p. 195; Cornelius Castoriadis, *World in Fragments*, p. 392.

23. Cornelius Castoriadis, *The Imaginary Institution*, p. 195.

24. Cornelius Castoriadis, *The Imaginary Institution* p. 185, emphasis added. For alternative discussions of Castoriadis's idea of creation *ex nihilo* see Suzi Adams, *Castoriadis's Ontology: Being and Creation*, New York, Fordham University Press, 2011; Jeff Klooger, 'From Nothing: Castoriadis and the Concept of Creation', *Critical Horizons*, vol. 12, no.1, 2011, pp. 29-47; Fabio Ciaramelli, 'The Self-presupposition of the Origin: Homage to Cornelius Castoriadis', *Thesis Eleven*, no. 49, 1997, pp. 45-67. Stathis Gourgouris, 'Autonomy and Self-alteration', in Ingrid S. Straume and Giorgio Baruchello (eds.), *Creation Rationality and Autonomy: Essays on Cornelius Castoriadis*, Copenhagen, Denmark, Aarhus University Press NSU, 2013, pp. 243-268 at pp. 248-250.

25. Stathis Gourgouris, 'Autonomy and Self-alteration', pp. 249-250.

This is why 'true time', the time of otherness-alteration, is at once a time of creation ex nihilo *and* destruction: 'time is being in so far as being is otherness, creation and destruction'.[26] The emergence of *eidos*, that is, new forms or determinations that are 'neither producible nor deducible from other forms' that are already there, so to speak, entails destruction given that every newly created form shatters determinacy in that it unavoidably 'alters the total form of what was there' before,[27] even though as Suzi Adams argues, this alteration, or (re)creation, must take place in unavoidably hermeneutical spaces.[28] The emergence of the idea of radical finitude within the western European world serves as an example of the process Castoriadis has in mind. As Angelos Mouzakitis shows, through his study of Greek thought (myth, philosophy and tragedy) Castoriadis attributes the emergence of humans' awareness of the inescapability of their death to certain aspects of Greek culture.[29] From this perspective, history itself is 'the emergence of otherness, immanent creation, non-trivial novelty'.[30]

History is what Castoriadis calls 'radical imaginary time', which is a dimension of both the social-historical imaginary and the radical imagination, imagination as a source of creation for the psychic subject.[31] As such, it is not a series of succeeding frameworks, rather it happens as different '*modes* of historicity'. That is, different societies actually institute socio-historical time in 'modalities according

---

26. Cornelius Castoriadis, *World in Fragments*, p. 395.

27. Cornelius Castoriadis, *World in Fragments*, pp. 392-395.

28. Suzi Adams, 'Interpreting Creation: Castoriadis and the birth of autonomy', *Thesis Eleven*, vol. 83, 2005, pp. 25-41 at p. 31.

29. Angelos Mouzakitis, 'Chaos and Creation in Castoriadis's Interpretation of Greek Thought', in Ingrid S. Straume and Giorgio Baruchello (eds.), *Creation Rationality and Autonomy: Essays on Cornelius Castoriadis*, Copenhagen, Denmark, Aarhus University Press, 2013, NSU, pp. 31-48 at pp. 37-43.

30. Cornelius Castoriadis, *The Imaginary Institution*, p. 184.

31. Cornelius Castoriadis, *The Imaginary Institution*, p. 193. See also Anthony Elliott, 'New Individualist Configurations and the Social Imaginary: Castoriadis and Kristeva', *European Journal of Social Theory*, vol. 15, no. 3, 2012, pp. 349- 365 at pp. 355-356.

to which [... they] represent and make their incessant self-alteration, even if in the extreme they deny it, or attempt to deny it'.[32] As well as an explicit 'identitary time immersed in a magma of imaginary significations', that is, as well as society's *explicit* instituted identitary time (calendar time) and its instituted social imaginary time (the time of signification), each society also has its way of *instituting* its own historical temporality.

> Every society exists by instituting the world as its world, or its world as the world and by instituting itself as part of this world. In this institution of the world and of society, by society, the institution of time is always an essential component.[33]

For example, in the contemporary world of capitalism, society's particular mode of self-alteration makes possible a certain range of institutions and significations. Whereas capitalist society's explicit institution of identitary time is that of 'a measurable, homogeneous, uniform and wholly arithmetizable flux', its imaginary time is typified by the 'infinite' represented as 'a time of indefinite progress, unlimited growth, accumulation, rationalization, the time of conquest of nature' and so on.[34] Yet this combination of identitary and imaginary time is not what capitalism *is* or *creates* as 'its own particular mode of historical temporality'.[35] Although it does not necessarily know or represent this to itself in this way, capitalism's time of creation manifests as a certain conflict between the explicit and implicit levels of its actuality: 'the time of incessant rupture, of recurrent catastrophes, of revolutions, of perpetually being torn away from what already exists' and 'the time of accumulation, of universal linearization, of digestion-assimilation, of making the dynamic static, of the effective suppression of otherness'.[36] Even though social-historical formations constitute

32. Cornelius Castoriadis, *The Imaginary Institution*, p. 185.
33. Cornelius Castoriadis, *The Imaginary Institution*, pp. 186–187.
34. Cornelius Castoriadis, *The Imaginary Institution*, p. 207.
35. Cornelius Castoriadis, *The Imaginary Institution*, p. 206.
36. Cornelius Castoriadis, *The Imaginary Institution*, p. 207.

'a specific way of making [as distinct from living] time',[37] to date, society has denied its self-instituting power.

Instituted society 'as we know it' is *heteronomous* in that its specific mode of self-institution fails to present itself as self-instituting.[38] For the most part society has not been able to recognize itself as its own origin and foundation: 'to see itself as creation, source of its institution, ever-present possibility of alteration of this institution; to recognize itself as always more and always also something other than *what* it is'.[39] Indeed, imaginary time instituted as the time of social representation 'always tends to cover over, to conceal and to deny temporality as otherness-alteration'.[40] The defining characteristic of heteronomous society is therefore its pervasive 'misrecognition [...] of its own being as creation and creativity'; its positing of its institution as beyond the reach of its own powers.[41]

> Everything occurs as if society had to [...] conceal its being as society by negating the temporality that is first and foremost its own temporality, the time of otherness-alteration [...] everything happens as if society were unable to recognize itself as making itself, as instituting itself as self-instituting.[42]

Yet for Castoriadis the social struggle to institute society *as self-instituting*, or in other words, the project of autonomy, is not undermined by the prolonged existence of heteronomous society. It remains a genuine possibility for humanity in light of the examples firstly of the institution of democracy in ancient Athens and secondly of the emergence in modern Europe of 'partially open societies [...] along with self-reflective individuals who are capable of critically distancing themselves from their society'.[43] In connection with the first

---

37. Cornelius Castoriadis, *World in Fragments*, p. 327.
38. Cornelius Castoriadis, *The Imaginary Institution*, pp. 213–214.
39. Cornelius Castoriadis, *World in Fragments*, p. 327.
40. Cornelius Castoriadis, *The Imaginary Institution*, p. 212.
41. Cornelius Castoriadis, *World in Fragments*, pp. 327–328.
42. Cornelius Castoriadis, *The Imaginary Institution*, p. 213.
43. Cornelius Castoriadis, *The Castoriadis Reader*, David Ames Curtis (ed.), Oxford, UK, Blackwell Publishers, 1997, pp. 336-337.

Gilles Labelle reads Castoriadis as follows.

> In breaking away from ['hetero-determined ...] schema,
> [...] Athenian democracy opens the door to the *explicit*
> self-institution of society. [...] the demos defined by the
> exclusion of slaves, metics and women demonstrates
> the limits of this form of democracy. Notwithstanding
> these limits, however, Athenian democracy is built upon
> a series of imaginary significations that render possible,
> for the first time, an infinite interrogation as to the in-
> stitution of Being and therefore a kind of permanent
> self-institution.[44]

Castoriadis analyzes Athenian democracy in terms of
the emergence of the principle of self-instituting activity. Nonetheless, Labelle argues that following the demise
of Athenian democracy whose rise Castoriadis considers a
kind of unpredictable 'breach' of heteronomous determinacy, 'the analyst can merely note the presence or absence of
the *demos* at any given moment in history'.[45] In other words,
it's not possible from this reflective standpoint to explain
neither the demise nor the emergence of an autonomous
society. Castoriadis admits that heteronomous society perpetuates the denial of its self-creation as a way of protect-
ing itself from the social Abyss, the Chaos that it is, but beyond this, society's heteronomy remains an enigma in that
we cannot say *why* society should have instituted itself as
heteronomous.[46] Yet he also believes that we, self-reflective
individuals of modernity, have no reason to accept the impossibility of a radical 'self-transformation of history' in the
sense of the creation of a *new mode* of instituting new institutions. Even though this presupposes the refutation of the
idea of an unavoidable structural heteronomy, he believes
this refutation to be evidenced in modern subject's political practice of *questioning* society's heteronomy in ways that

---

44. Gilles Labelle, 'Two Refoundation Projects of Democracy in
Contemporary French Philosophy: Cornelius Castoriadis and Jacques
Rancière', *Philosophy and Social Criticism*, vol. 27, no. 4. 2001, pp. 75-103
at p. 80.

45. Gilles Labelle, 'Two Refoundation Projects', pp. 82-83.

46. Cornelius Castoriadis, *World in Fragments*, p. 328.

produce partial ruptures (hereafter 'revolutionary agency').[47] We turn next to outline Castoriadis's understanding of the nature of this practice and the formative conditions of the associated political agency.

POLITICS AND DEMOCRACY

Being underpinned by self-reflective individuals' capacity to question instituted society, the project of political autonomy seeks, first and foremost, to (re)institute the *demos* as a genuine democracy. As Gerasimos Karavitis points out, for Castoriadis, democracy need not take the form of state; it is 'the *kratos* in which the transformative thrust of politics becomes a norm secured in the last instance by explicit power'.[48] Democracy is 'the regime of explicit and lucid self-institution, as far as is possible, of the social institutions that depend on explicit collective activity' and whose establishment is essential to the success of the project of an autonomous society.[49] It is in short 'the project of breaking the closure [of meaning] at the collective level'.[50]

> If the law is God-given, or if there is a philosophical or scientific 'grounding' of substantive political truths (with Nature, Reason, or History as ultimate 'principle') then there exists an extra-social standard for society. There is a norm of the norm, a law of the law, a criterion on the basis of which the question of whether a particular law (or state of affairs), is just or unjust, proper or improper, can be discussed and decided. This criterion is

47. Cornelius Castoriadis, *The Imaginary Institution*, p. 373; *World in Fragments*, pp.328–329.

48. Gerasimos Karavitis, 'On the Concept of Politics' p. 260.

49. Cornelius Castoriadis, 'Democracy as Procedure and Democracy as Regime', *Constellations*, vol. 4, no. 1, 1997, pp. 1-18, at pp. 4-5.

50. Cornelius Castoriadis, *Philosophy Politics Autonomy*, p. 21. For a recent discussion of the significance of closure in Castoriadis's theory see Jeff Klooger, 'Plurality and Indeterminacy: Revisiting Castoriadis's overly Homogeneous Conception of Society', *European Journal of Social Theory*, 2011, pp. 1-17.

given once and for all and, *ex hypothesi*, does not depend upon human action.

Once it is recognized that no such ground exists, either because there is a separation between religion and politics, as is, imperfectly, the case in modern societies, or because, as in Greece, religion is kept strictly at bay by political activities, and once it is also recognized that there is no 'science', no *επιστήμη* or *τέχνη*,of political matters, the question of what a just law is, what justice is—what the 'proper' institution of society is—opens up as a genuine, that is, *interminable question.*[51]

For Castoriadis then, precisely because 'a society is autonomous not only when it knows that it makes its laws but also if it is up to the task of putting them into question,'[52] the availability of such questioning is the mark of a genuine democracy.

As with the political practice of the Athenians, a genuinely democratic regime must give effect to the universally valid distinction between three spheres of activity. According to Castoriadis,

the overall institution of society must both separate and articulate: the *oikos*, the *agora*, and the *ekkle-sia*. A free translation would be: the private sphere, the private/public sphere, and the (formally and in the strong sense) public sphere, identical to [...] explicit power.[53]

A genuinely democratic regime establishes an autonomous sphere of politics in the sense of political activity (*la politique*), as distinct from taking for granted the already instituted framework of the political life of society (*le politique*).[54] It is therefore 'the regime in which the public sphere becomes truly and effectively publicbelongs to everyone, is effectively open to the participation of all' in and as 'the *ekkle-sia*', Castoriadis's term for the public/public sphere, that

51. Cornelius Castoriadis, 'The Greek *Πόλις*', p. 50, emphasis added.

52. Cornelius Castoriadis, *World in Fragments*, p. 87.

53. Cornelius Castoriadis,'Democracy as Procedure', p. 7.

54. Cornelius Castoriadis, *Philosophy Politics Autonomy*, p. 158-162; Cornelius Castoriadis,'Democracy as Procedure', p. 1.

is, the site of the political or, in other words, explicit power.[55] A just regime is therefore defined by the openness of 'public time' and 'public space'.[56]

Moreover, the institution of society must be capable of making democratic procedures function in accordance with their egalitarian participatory spirit and this in turn calls for the cultivation of democratic citizens with the capacity for self-limitation. For this,

> the institution of society must endow critical thinking as such with positive value—and then the Pandora's box of putting existing institutions into question is opened up and democracy again becomes society's movement of self-institution—that is to say, a new type of regime in the full sense of the term.[57]

For Castoriadis, the cultivation of such critical thinking is a matter of 'true *paideia* ':

> We want autonomous individuals, that is, individuals capable of self-reflective activity. But unless we are to enter into an endless repetition, the contents and the objects of this activity, even the developments of its means and methods, must be supplied by the radical imagination. [...] this is why a non-mutilating education, a true *paideia*, is of paramount importance.[58]

Ingrid Straume suggests *paideia* is 'tied to the socialisation processes whereby the human psyche internalises the social institution' and through it the pursuit of autonomy becomes 'thinkable and makes sense' in so far as this idea forms part of a society's central imaginary significations, or in other

55. Cornelius Castoriadis, 'Democracy as Procedure', pp. 7-8. Compare contemporary discussions of 'the public sphere', which can be used to refer to 'at least three analytically distinct things: the state, the official economy of paid employment and arenas of public discourse': Nancy Fraser, 'Rethinking the Public Sphere' in Simon During (ed.), *The Cultural Studies Reader*, London and New York, Routledge, Second edition, 1993, pp. 516-536 at p. 519.

56. Cornelius Castoriadis, 'The Greek Πόλις and the Creation of Democracy' in *The Ancients and the Moderns*, R. Lily, (ed,), Bloomington, Indiana, Indiana University Press, 1996, pp. 29-58 at p. 49.

57. Cornelius Castoriadis, 'Democracy as Procedure', p. 10.

58. Cornelius Castoriadis, *World in Fragments*, p. 133.

words, so long as it belongs to a society's 'radical ground power'.[59] Castoriadis maintains this power, understood as the all-pervasive undifferentiated determining force of instituted society, 'is grounded upon the instituting power of the radical imaginary'. It is something that every society produces and 'wields over individuals' '[b]efore any explicit power and, even more, before any "domination" of the institution of society'.[60] This is why the idea of autonomy must already belong to a society's radical ground power as a precondition for the former's pursuit and enactment, whether by individuals or collectives. Harald Wolf argues that at this level the difference between autonomous and heteronomous power concerns the conspicuous absence of power qua power, though not qua effects of power, in the case of heteronomy. By contrast autonomous power 'has as its aim the greatest possible *presence* of infra-power [or ground power]; it is the permanent attempt to make the power of the imaginary visible'.[61] For Karavitis the conservation effect of radical ground-power aligns it with Castoriadis' concept of the political, and yet it is a mode of instituting power. In a genuine democracy radical groundpower therefore has 'a paradoxical status':

> it fabricates individuals capable of putting the conservation of their society—and thus the effects of radical groundpower itself—into question. It constructs social individuals capable of resisting the uncritical reduplication of their own society, even though it is democratic.[62]

It follows from the above that radical democratic participation, inalienable access of each individual to society's explicit power, gives rise to the possibility of creating the new as a genuine project for humanity precisely because 'the origin,

59. Ingrid S. Straume, 'Castoriadis, Education and Democracy', in Ingrid S. Straume and Giorgio Baruchello (eds.), *Creation Rationality and Autonomy: Essays on Cornelius Castoriadis*, Copenhagen, Denmark, Aarhus University Press NSU, 2013, pp. 203-228 at p. 219.

60. Cornelius Castoriadis, *Philosophy Politics Autonomy*, 2013, p. 150.

61. Harald Wolf 'The Power of the Imaginary', in Ingrid S. Straume and Giorgio Baruchello (eds.), *Creation Rationality and Autonomy: Essays on Cornelius Castoriadis*, Copenhagen, Denmark, Aarhus University Press NSU, 2013, pp. 185-201 at p. 197.

62. Gerasimos Karavitis, 'On the Concept of Politics', pp. 258-260.

the cause, the foundation of society is society itself, as instituting society'.[63] This is what Castoriadis means in claiming that 'society as such is self-creation'.[64] In the present context creation, in the radical sense of ontological creation *ex nihilo,* means 'the positing of a new *eidos,* a new essence, a new form in the full and strong sense: new determinations, new norms, new laws'.[65] On Karavitis's reading, 'the advent of the new occurs [...] as the hitherto unpredictable redirection of cathexis' through which democratic subjects assign 'a new value' to existing significations.[66]

Significantly, 'the institutions and social imaginary significations of each society are the creations of the anonymous collective concerned', that is, 'the people' in the broad sense of this term.[67]

> We cannot conceive such creation as the work of the one or of a few individuals who might be designated by name, but only as that of the collective-anonymous imaginary, of the instituting imaginary, to which, in this regard, we shall give the name instituting power'.[68]

For Castoriadis, politics proper, understood as 'explicit and lucid activity that concerns the instauration of desirable institutions',[69] calls upon the anonymous collective to create by *incessantly* questioning the already instituted and not sim-

---

63. Cornelius Castoriadis,'Democracy as Procedure', p. 10; Cornelius Castoriadis, *World in Fragments,* p. 327.

64. Cornelius Castoriadis, *World in Fragments,* p. 333.

65. Cornelius Castoriadis, 'The Greek *Πόλις*', p. 31.

66. Gerasimos Karavitis, 'On the Concept of Politics', p. 259. For a comparison of Castoriadis and Arendt regarding political creation of the new see Ingrid S. Straume, 'A Common World: Arendt Castoriadis and Political Creation', *European Journal of Social Theory,* vol. 15, no. 3, 2012, pp. 367-383; Linda MG Zerilli, 'Castoriadis Arendt and the Problem of the New', *Constellations,* vol. 9, no. 2., 2002, pp. 540-553.

67. Cornelius Castoriadis, *World in Fragments,* p. 333. Cornelius Castoriadis, *The Castoriadis Reader,* p. 322. For a discussion of the difference between Castoriadis's conception of the 'anonymous collective' and the political 'autonomous collective' in Castoriadis's thought see Andreas Kalyvas, 'The Radical Instituting Power and Democratic Theory' *Journal of the Hellenic Diaspora,* vol. 24, no. 1, 1998, pp. 9-29.

68. Cornelius Castoriadis, *World in Fragments,* p. 84.

69. Cornelius Castoriadis,'Democracy as Procedure', p. 4.

ply to create and endorse the just institutions once and for all. For the anonymous collective then the specific characteristics of just institutions cannot be pre-determined philosophically. For example, we could not arrive at a definitive account of the basic structure of just institutions through reflection behind a veil of ignorance, or some other thought experiment, because such determinations ultimately rely on pre-conceived ideas of the common good whereas 'the question of the common good belongs to the domain of social-historical making/doing [*faire*] not to theory'.[70] Rather, in the incessant practice of (re)creating the institutions of a just democracy the anonymous collective must therefore be guided by an open-ended criterion.

> The laws and institutions of a democratic society give rise to the political imperative 'create the institutions that, by being internalized by individuals, most facilitate their accession to their individual autonomy and their effective participation in all forms of explicit power existing in society'.[71]

For radical democratic subjects this formulation of the *telos* of democratic society gives determinate shape to the democratic process by linking participation to the radical imaginary power of the collective.

> In this context 'imaginary' [...] does not signify the 'fictive', the 'illusory', the 'specular', but rather the positing of new forms. This positing is not determined but rather determining; it is an unmotivated positing.[72]

It is the *constituting element* of political autonomy—the

---

70. Cornelius Castoriadis,'Democracy as Procedure', p. 15.

71. Cornelius Castoriadis, *Philosophy Politics Autonomy*, p. 173. Wolf reads this political imperative as 'the attempt of a conscious appropriation of the social infra-power [or ground-power]—as far as possible—to turn it into explicit power, available in an egalitarian way' for '[a]s long as the [...] image of the social institution remains [...] underneath/below our perception limit, we stick to a heteronomous state. Then we remain subject to its power. We must raise it beyond the social perception threshold—open it to reflection and the appropriating, transforming praxis. The autonomy project implies the raising beyond those limits.' Harald Wolf 'The Power of the Imaginary', pp. 192-193.

72. Cornelius Castoriadis, *World in Fragments*, p. 84.

definition of autonomy in terms of society's explicit self-instituting power—that, as Andreas Kalyvas observes, enables a potential re-inscription of the democratic process.[73]

Castoriadis recognizes that 'the equal effective participation of all in society's effective power to posit the law presupposes deep intervention in the substantive organisation of social life'.[74] Democracy is therefore a movement for greater appropriations of the instituting social imaginary ground-power 'with a view towards transforming the instituted capitalist relations of domination and inequality'.[75] To achieve such a transformation is at the very least to institute new ideas of publicness as was the case in the Athenian *polis*. The life of the Athenian *polis* gives rise to the creation of a 'public space' to which 'only the education *(παιδεία)* of the citizens as citizens can give valuable substantive content' and to 'the creation of a public time', meaning 'the emergence of a dimension where the collectivity can inspect its own past, as the result of its own actions, and where an indeterminate future opens up a domain for its activities'.[76] Accordingly, as a project that expresses and embodies political autonomy, democracy aspires to 'break the closure at the collective level'.[77]

RADICAL DEMOCRATIC POLITICS IN NEO-LIBERAL TIMES

Castoriadis's idea of radical democratic politics has been praised for its potential to redefine the democratic process in terms that steer clear of the familiar problems associated with contemporary liberal and neo-Kantian proceduralism, on the one hand, and neo-Aristotelian communitarianism, on the other. For example, Kalyvas has shown that

73. See Andreas Kalyvas, 'The Radical Instituting Power'.

74. Cornelius Castoriadis, 'Democracy as Procedure', p. 6.

75. Andreas Kalyvas, 'The Radical Instituting Power', p. 22.

76. Cornelius Castoriadis, 'The Greek *Πόλις*', p. 49.

77. Cornelius Castoriadis, *Philosophy Politics Autonomy*, pp. 20-21;Cornelius Castoriadis, *The Castoriadis Reader*, pp. 336-337.

by drawing on the idea of the autonomous political creation of institutions that facilitate a shared public ethos of participation, Castoriadis's understanding of the political project of autonomy resists reliance on either an empty formalistic procedure that invokes impartiality and pseudo-neutrality of the sort he attributes to contemporary theorists of deliberative democracy or a pre-given essentialist content informing the democratic process.[78] Yet, contemporary critiques of the meaning and ideological uses of western conceptualizations of democracy pose new challenges. Notably, in a collection of essays devoted to uncovering the (misplaced) authority of the word 'democracy', Wendy Brown objects to democracy's presumption 'that human beings want to be self-legislating'. She also observes, 'when non-democrats are housed in shells of democracies' this gives rise to the possibility of 'fascism authored by the people'.[79]

> On the one side, then, we face the problem of peoples who do not aspire to democratic freedom and, on the other, of democracies we do not want [...] Contouring both possibilities is the problem of peoples oriented towards short-run gratifications [...] and disinclined to sacrifice either their pleasures or their hatreds for collective thriving.[80]

Moreover, against the privileging of democratic practices, we may also cite First Nations that place democratic processes within an ontological framework that prioritizes the authority of Law. For example, speaking from a 'critical Indigenous standpoint', Irene Watson explains 'the way of the future belongs to First Nations laws to determine, interpret and translate' and this indicates a certain groundedness through ongoing connection to country that cannot be substituted for

---

78. See Andreas Kalyvas, 'The Radical Instituting Power'; 'The Politics of Autonomy'.

79. Wendy Brown, 'We are all Democrats Now ...' in Giorgio Agamben, Alain Badiou, Daniel Bensaid, Wendy Brown, Jean-Luc Nancy, Jacques Rancière, Kristin Ross, and Slavoj Žižek, trans. William McCuaig, *Democracy in What State?* New York, Columbia University Press, 2012, pp. 44-57 at pp. 54-55.

80. Wendy Brown, 'We are all Democrats Now ...', pp. 55-56.

the openendedness of radical democratic questioning:

> Authority is in the hands of First Nations Peoples and is law [...] Our future lies in following proper lines of authority that derive from ancient laws, laws which are still carried and known to First Nations Peoples, our territories and the worlds we occupy.[81]

Like Brown, Alain Badiou voices concerns about the consumerist conceptions of democratic subjectivity that now dominate in western liberal societies. He insists that having been trained in a democracy wherein 'everything is equivalent to everything else', the democratic subject of western capitalist societies

> reflects the substitutability of everything for everything else. So we have the overt circulation of desires, of the objects on which these desires fix, and of the cheap thrills they deliver, and it's within this circulation that the subject is constituted.[82]

Echoing Plato's critique of the democratic character in *The Republic* to which we will return in Chapter 5, Badiou suggests that 'the only thing that constitutes the democratic subject is pleasure or, more precisely, pleasure-seeking behaviour'.[83]

Castoriadis would of course agree with the observations underpinning this critique of so-called democracy as currently lived, especially representative liberal democracies whose form he considers to be oligarchic.[84] In paradoxically privatizing the public, today's heteronomous societies misrepresent themselves; they are in fact 'pseudo-democracies'.[85]

---

81. Irene Watson, 'First Nations, Indigenous Peoples: Our Laws Have Always Been Here', in Irene Watson (ed.), *Indigenous Peoples as Subjects of International Law*, Routledge, EBook Central, 2017, p. 97.

82. Alain Badiou, 'The Democratic Emblem' in Giorgio Agamben, Alain Badiou, Daniel Bensaid, Wendy Brown, Jean-Luc Nancy, Jacques Rancière, Kristin Ross, and Slavoj Žižek, trans. William McCuaig, *Democracy in What State?* New York, Columbia University Press, 2012, pp. 6-15 at pp. 10-11.

83. Alain Badiou, 'The Democratic Emblem', p. 9.

84. For discussion of Castoriadis on contemporary liberal oligarchies see Christophe Premat, 'Castoriadis and the Modern Political Imaginary'.

85. Cornelius Castoriadis,'Democracy as Procedure', p. 7. See also

At the level of cultural critique, Anthony Elliott observes that Castoriadis deploys an underdeveloped notion of 'generalized conformism' to describe the times.[86] Nonetheless Castoriadis laments today's absence of a passion for public affairs, the deep desire for responsible institution-making that is indispensable for establishment a genuine democracy[87]. For Castoriadis, with political apathy linked to the privatization of the public sphere and capitalism's reinforcement of consumerism, things have 'become worthless'.[88] Currently,

> without any conspiracy by some power that one could designate, everything conspires, in the sense of radiating in the same direction, for the same results, that is to say, insignificance.[89]

Yet despite 'the spirit of the times' favouring 'insignificance', it does not follow that there is no scope for practicing the kind of critical reflection Castoriadis would associate with radical democratic subjects in pursuit of autonomy. Castoriadis takes the view that the human potential for autonomy is not

---

Cornelius Castoriadis, 'The Dilapidation of the West', *Thesis Eleven*, vol. 41, no. 1, 1995, pp. 94-111. But see also Christophe Premat who argues that since contemporary political regimes described as representative democracies function as 'liberal oligarchies', Castoriadis's rejection of representational democracy is arguably too quick. For Premat the principle of representation allows for the 'accountability of people who are in charge of collective duties': Christophe Premat, 'Castoriadis and the Modern Political Imaginary', p. 270.

86. Anthony Elliott, 'New Individualist Configurations', p.357.

87. Cornelius Castoriadis, *World in Fragments*, p. 39.

88. Cornelius Castoriadis, *Postscript on Insignificance*, Gabriel Rockhill (ed.), Gabriel Rockhill and John V Garner (trans.), New York, Continuum, 2011, p. 6.

89. Cornelius Castoriadis, *Postscript on Insignificance*, p.6. See also Cornelius Castoriadis, *Figures of the Thinkable*, trans. Helen Arnold, Stanford, CA, Stanford University Press, 2007, p. 66. Wolf reads this diagnosis as referring 'particularly to the erosion of values, norms, social roles, which seemed up until now necessary for the functioning of the [liberal capitalist] system': Harald Wolf, 'The power of the imaginary', p. 200. See also Labelle, 'Two Refoundation Projects', p.85. As we explain in detail in Chapters 3 and 4, for our purposes the absence of such significations is noteworthy, not because they no longer orient subjects towards liberal capitalist values but for their failure to orient subjects towards what we referred to in Chapter 1 as significant communality.

restricted by society. As socialized beings, individuals do not exist in opposition to the social since 'the institution produces in conformity with its norms, individuals that by construction are not only able but bound to reproduce the institution'.[90] Instead, certain social imaginary institutions give rise to autonomous subjects. As we noted above, Karavitis argues that in naming a transformative force politics is linked to the cathectic practices of the psyche. So 'the redirection of cathexis is, for Castoriadis, the necessary and sufficient condition of radical transformation'.[91] The Castoriadian differentiation of the concepts of (autonomous instituting) politics and the (heteronomous instituted) political thereby marks the point of transition from heteronomous to autonomous society, since heteronomous societies 'render politics impossible or undesirable or 'reduce it to an effect of the political, while autonomous societies 'secure conditions for politics'. While appeal to the difference between politics and the political goes some way towards accounting for radical social transformation, it still leaves unanswered the question of the conditions informing such change. How does the current neo-liberalism inform such processes?

Reflecting from a Castoriadian perspective, Sophie Klimis considers the broader question of the effects of neoliberal times on the constitution of subjectivity. As she points out, Castoriadis would agree that today's young people are educated into a culture for the pursuit of enjoyment without frustration of any kind, so much so that there is no reason to invest in socially useful collective significations. Klimis argues that this awareness also leads Castoriadis to present a 'new anthropological type'. She notices that Castoriadis' characterization of the neo-liberal individual resembles 'his descriptions of the monadic core of the primal subject: self-centred, all-powerful, asocial and antisocial, always searching for pleasure and satisfaction'. Klimis also suggests that what is missing from this 'social *analoga*' of Castoriadis' description of the primal subject is the

---

90. Cornelius Castoriadis, *World in Fragments*, p. 7.
91. Gerasimos Karavitis, 'On the Concept of Politics', pp. 257-259.

'unlimited activity of the imagination'. The question therefore arises:

> Has this society produced a kind of individual that re-
> sembles the monadic psyche, but which, *being a social
> creation*, is not able to reactivate the imaginative poten-
> tial of that monad? In other words, instead of socializing
> human beings the effect of the neoliberal capitalist so-
> cial imaginary is to dehumanize us, subverting the pro-
> cess of socialization from within through individuals'
> loss of the power of radical imagination, ultimately lead-
> ing to 'social self-destruction.[92]

If Klimis's reading is well founded, then there is no reason to expect the emergence of revolutionary agency under
present conditions. However, following Gourgouris, we may
read Castoriadis's notion of the radical imagination as operating as a capacity of the human psyche 'at the level of
drives' and not as a kind of '*cultural* capacity'.[93] Accordingly,
it may not be *loss* of the power of radical imagination but
rather its misdirection, in being a self-imposed dehuman-
ization to which Klimis's analysis of neoliberal subjectivity points. This would still leave open the question of the
emergence of *autonomous subjectivity* out of the conditions
of a heteronomous social order of the sort we are experiencing under neo-liberal capitalism. In response to the broader
question, Gourgouris concedes

> [i]t is unclear what social-historical conditions are
> needed for subjectification to take this form [autonomy].
> [...] It can only emerge as the praxis/*poiesis* within a cer-
> tain social-imaginary, which surely does not mean that
> it is the mere expression or application of a certain so-
> cial imaginary.[94]

Let us return to Straume's analysis of Castoriadis's concept
of democratic *paideia, that is,* the socialization of individuals in a genuine democracy. Straume suggests that, despite

92. Sophie Klimis, 'From Modernity to Neoliberalism: What Human
Subject?', in Ingrid S. Straume and Giorgio Baruchello (eds.), *Creation
Rationality and Autonomy: Essays on Cornelius Castoriadis*, Copenhagen,
Denmark, Aarhus University Press NSU, 2013, pp. 133-158 at pp. 148-149.

93. Stathis Gourgouris, 'Autonomy and Self-alteration', p. 255.

94. Stathis Gourgouris, 'Autonomy and Self-alteration', p. 266.

being underdeveloped, this notion provides insight into subjects' self-transformation from heteronomy to autonomy, which is effectively, the production of individuals 'who are different than ourselves and the society in which they are produced', by 'the existing—and at least partly undesirable institutions'. According to Straume, the happening of the paradox of depending on the institution for one's constitution as a subject capable of calling that institution into question, involves an inexplicable 'leap' of the sort that also 'takes place when the social-historical and the individuals change simultaneously'. She concludes, '[t]he paradox cannot be solved by logic, only acted out as a creation, a political act'. Indeed, in relation to those whose autonomy is 'not yet fully developed', Straume draws on Castoriadis's discussion of psychoanalysis to conclude, '[a]ll we can do, according to Castoriadis, is to act *as if*, and make use of the autonomy that is not yet fully developed.'[95] We turn next to consider Castoriadis' association of autonomy with willing singularities.

95. Ingrid S, Straume, 'Castoriadis, Education and Democracy', pp. 224-226.

3. RADICAL WILLING,
THE CHAOS OF SIGNIFICANCE
AND THE ABYSS OF INSIGNIFICANCE

The self-transformation of society concerns social doing—and so also politics, in the profound sense of the term—the doing of men and women in society, and nothing else. Of this, thoughtful doing, and political thinking—society's thinking as making itself—is one essential component.[96]

For Castoriadis 'thoughtful doing, and political thinking' are at the heart of radical politics. They are the conceptual epicentre of a state of awareness focused on 'society's thinking as making itself' or time as creation in the terms already outlined. As such they perform a visionary role in opening the political and conceptual spaces for an *autonomous way of thinking/being*. In thinking the socio-historical in and as its self-making, Castoriadis's own thought aspires to autonomous thinking, which in bringing the new into being creates its own time. After all, he takes social doing, in general, and thoughtful doing and political thinking in particular, to be closer to true temporality than the time of social representation since, the time of doing is co-extensive with the time of creation and, as we noted earlier, it is the time of creation that makes possible the emergence of genuine alterity.[97]

96. Cornelius Castoriadis, *The Imaginary Institution*, p. 373.
97. Cornelius Castoriadis, *The Imaginary Institution*, p. 212.

AUTONOMOUS THINKING AS VISIONARY PRACTICE

If Castoriadis is in a position to think the project of autonomy this is because and in so far as he finds himself awakened by the otherness of thinking autonomously. For, we 'experience otherness the moment we fall in love [...], or with any sudden change of mood, or in the emergence of another idea.'[98] In its capacity as the emergence of 'another idea', the above-mentioned claim regarding society's self-making through thoughtful doing and political thinking points to the openness of the project of (thinking and democratically practicing) autonomy, to the commitment to its unceasing self-questioning and reformulation. As we have seen, Castoriadis does not just want to present an alternative theory to someone who would question or problematize an intellectual path while remaining within the conceptual confines of identitary thought. Nor can his intellectual practice be characterized by an impartial mode of reasoning from given premises—anthropological, logical, ontological and so on—or even by the desire to give a description of its objects of inquiry—society, specific socio-historical formations or human subjects—where these are taken as given and as indifferent to the thinking that takes place with respect to them. Rather, the thinking that Castoriadis performs should be understood in terms of an unfolding of thinking itself, that which unceasingly engages in making its own time, *the time of its knowing, being and becoming* in creating *eidos*. Already in producing *The Imaginary Institution of Society* the thinker's intellectual practice becomes the vision of the possibility of a thinkingly-created social-historical reality. Castoriadis's intellectual practice should be taken to exemplify 'society's thinking as making itself'.

The above reference to the visionary character of Castoriadis's thinking is not an appeal to a future that is not yet. Instead, it characterizes the thinker's *present* practice in its vibrant, self-altering movement:

---

98. Cornelius Castoriadis, *World in Fragments*, p. 394.

the time of otherness-alteration is a time of bursting, emerging, creating. The present, the *nun*, is here explosion, split, rupture—the rupture of what is as such. This present exists as originating, as immanent transcendence, as source, as the surging forth of ontological genesis.[99]

So Castoriadis's visionary stance is a way of appreciating the radical openness of the future in the present in which he finds himself, the present as the activity of the 'surging forth' of the creation of new ideas, which is in stark contrast to the 'repetition of identitary presents' that characterize the homogeneous thinking that is the usual practice of inherited thought.[100]

Moreover, radical social transformation must stem from the activity of the sort of alert creative thinking we have outlined above with one important proviso. Its fundamentals take shape through the *collective* practices of individuals. This is the power of thought not only to be shared by the thinking singularities who make up the anonymous collective, but also through this sharing to transform itself into a formed world of institutions.[101]

In the final paragraph of *The Imaginary Institution of Society* Castoriadis contrasts *the genuine place* of radical autonomy with what he calls the fictive *'non-place* of identitary logic-ontology'.[102] The latter is the basis on which it becomes possible to deny the self-transformation of history towards a new explicitly self-instituting mode of instituted society. This 'place'/'non-place' distinction also informs alternative modes of engaging the singularity of the thinker. On the one hand, with its appetite for laws and causal explanations of the social-historical based on pre-given concepts and logical processes, the heteronomous thinking of 'non-place' is precisely the sort of thinking that, as we noted above, Castoriadis attributes to the inherited tradition. In contrast,

99. Cornelius Castoriadis, *The Imaginary Institution*, pp. 200–201.

100. Cornelius Castoriadis, *The Imaginary Institution*, p. 200.

101. Cornelius Castoriadis, *The Castoriadis Reader*, p. 389.

102. Cornelius Castoriadis, *The Imaginary Institution*, p. 373, emphasis added.

the only 'place' for the genuine thinker is that of affirming the viability of the project of autonomy. This, we want to suggest, is the place of radical willing, the commitment to being/becoming a *willing* singularity. For Castoriadis 'will or deliberative activity is the reflexive dimension of what we are as imaginative beings'.[103] This dimension of the subject's radical imagination is the capacity to intervene reflectively in its self-making, which in turn enables a focus on creating ruptures and revolutionary breaks.[104] Accordingly, Castoriadis links the possibility of a 'supersession' of heteronomous society to the thoughtful doing and political thinking of those who aim at the

> radical destruction of the known institution of society [...] because *we will it* and because *we know that others will it as well*, not because such are the laws of history, the interests of the proletariat or the destiny of being'.[105]

Notice here that in willing the project of autonomy, Castoriadis's political agents come together through their knowledge of one another and it is through this awareness that their shared practices gain their transformational power. In other words, they appear as a group of like-minded individuals whose reflective togetherness takes shape as an overlapping consensus of sorts.[106]

---

103. Cornelius Castoriadis, cited in Sophie Klimis, 'From Modernity to Neoliberalism', p. 142. See also Andreas Kalyvas, 'The Politics of Autonomy', p. 9.

104. Cornelius Castoriadis, *World in Fragments*, p. 160. See also Andreas Kalyvas, 'The Politics of Autonomy', p. 13.

105. Cornelius Castoriadis, *The Imaginary Institution*, p. 373.

106. Here we refer to a mode of consensus that draws on monological reflection in that the reasoning involved is not necessarily intersubjectively mediated at the level of giving determinate shape to an idea, but only at the level of confirmation of collective commitment to such idea. A contemporary example of an overlapping consensus in this sense is that formulated by the John Rawls of *Political Liberalism*, Columbia University Press, 1993. As Toula Nicolacopoulos argues in *The Radical Critique of Liberalism: In Memory of a Vision*, Melbourne, re.press, 2008, p. 190, such an overlapping consensus refers to the endorsement of an idea individually by the society's politically active citizens from the respective perspectives of their different and, perhaps opposing, reasonable convictions, which nonetheless form an essential constituent part of the idea that they each

It follows from the above that the place where the champion of radical autonomy stands, so to speak, is specified by the commitment of a *willing singularity* to deploy alterity. Presumably it is this sort of commitment that liberates the anonymous collective from social givens, those aspects of the socially fabricated individual that inhibit development of the desire for political autonomy and opens up the possibility of a non-identitary thinking, of the autonomous creation of *eidos*. In courageously willing the project of autonomy, we are in a position to confront and not be overwhelmed by the Chaos of society and of the world, the Abyss that is 'the no-place against which every place stands out'.[107] Although Castoriadis does not provide any concrete examples from the contemporary world, his description of the subject's relationship to the Groundless appears as the source of both joy and the weight of responsibility for the creative/destructive power of the radical imaginary. On this account the very moment it is experienced, radical willing becomes co-extensive with activating the visionary practice of autonomy. For Castoriadis, thought orients itself towards itself as a (potentially) material force of socio-historical doing by aspiring to a public sharing amongst like-minded individuals who are aware of society's self-instituting power.

It follows that society can become knowingly self-instituting—as the combination of its unceasing creation and the institutions thus created—through autonomous activity of the sort that Castoriadis's own intellectual practice seeks to exemplify in contrast to inherited thought that is founded on 'the concealment of doing and of bringing into being' and is therefore 'unaware of its own nature as *thoughtful doing*'.[108] Castoriadis's intervention is a matter of both

---

affirm. Compare Andreas Kalyvas, 'The Politics of Autonomy', pp. 9-10. In comparing Castoriadian and Habermasian conceptions of democratic *decision-making procedures*—as distinct from democratic citizens' critical reflections in and around such procedures—Kalyvas draws attention to Castoriadis's conception of the collective will as irreducible to the singular will.

107. Cornelius Castoriadis, *World in Fragments*, p. 325.
108. Cornelius Castoriadis, *The Imaginary Institution*, p. 373.

'thoughtful doing and political thinking' in the above sense of placing itself in the public arena in which it emerges as the initial, fundamental step towards achieving the project of autonomy. In other words, with his own intellectual practice Castoriadis aspires to render explicit 'society's thinking as making itself' by activating the very mode of being of the autonomous singularity who is, at once, the vision of an autonomous collective of individuals—the (in principle) gathering of society in its historical becoming within the horizon of the emerging vision—and the bringing into being or making of time that happens at the level of instituting society. We will refer to this practice as 'the visionary practice of autonomy' and to the thinker's aspiration as that of 'the champion of radical autonomy'.

We have suggested thus far that Castoriadis does not aim *to convince* in the sense of reaching an unavoidable conclusion, as might be the case when practising heteronomous modes of thinking. His philosophizing does not appeal to the *rational-logical* aspects of our socio-historical context, those aspects that might be open to the force of the better argument. Rather, in linking its transformative powers and in turn the very essence of the social-historical to a certain way of responding to heteronomous modes of being and thinking, it presents itself as a profound exercise in radical autonomy. This raises the question 'how does the champion of radical autonomy activate the visionary practice of autonomy?' To appreciate Castoriadis's answer, we must turn to his discussion of the nature and role of the Chaos, the Abyss, or Groundless of society and the world.

THE CHAOS OF SOCIETY AND WORLD

According to Castoriadis in every way 'humanity continues, prolongs, recreates the Chaos, the Abyss, the Groundless from which it emerges'.[109] Here 'Chaos' does not refer to

---

109. Cornelius Castoriadis, *World in Fragments*, p. 316.

a mere passive condition, an absence of determination. Castoriadis's idea of the 'Chaos' calls forth the double meaning of both void and 'embracing-nurturing abyss', as Angelos Mouzakitis argues drawing on Castoriadis's reading of 'the Greek conception of the world from Homer to classical antiquity'.[110] In Castoriadis's words, the Chaos is

> an unfathomable underside [*envers*] to everything [...] It is perpetual source, ever immanent alteration, [...] It is literally temporality [in the ontological sense of time] that is creation/destruction, time as alterity/alteration.[111]

Humanity continues and recreates the Chaos 'as the Groundlessness of the psyche's radical imagination' and as 'social Abyss, the Groundlessness of the [signifying and instituting] social imaginary'.[112] At the same time 'the labour of signification', that is, the creation of a proper world of meaning through which everything is in principle capable of being interpreted, is 'perpetually menaced [...] by the Chaos it encounters, by the Chaos it itself dredges up'.[113] Just as the socially fabricated individual is a thin yet ever-present film that covers over the psyche's Chaos, so too instituted society cannot 'totally cover over the Chaos' of the world.[114] In positing itself as total, as covering everything, signification runs the risk of not being able to deal with the Chaos, yet the Chaos is revealed in the perpetual struggle of heteronomous society to cover over both its own and the world's Chaos. The Chaos 'announces itself and asserts itself' through this unsuccessful effort at concealment.[115]

Accordingly, if true time, radical self-alteration, is capable of bringing itself into being in and through the announcement of the Chaos of society and the world, Groundlessness must be the condition of possibility of radical autonomous thinking. In other words, the intellectual practice of the

110. Angelos Mouzakitis, 'Chaos and Creation', p. 35. See also Sophie Klimis, 'From Modernity to Neoliberalism' p. 151.

111. Cornelius Castoriadis, *World in Fragments*, p. 322.

112. Cornelius Castoriadis, *World in Fragments*, p. 316.

113. Cornelius Castoriadis, *World in Fragments*, p. 313.

114. Cornelius Castoriadis, *World in Fragments*, p. 311–312.

115. Cornelius Castoriadis, *World in Fragments*, p. 316.

champion of radical autonomy can be neither motivated nor activated in the absence of a primordial awareness of the Chaos, the Abyss or the Groundlessness of society and the world. In its self-enactment as the visionary practice of autonomy in the terms outlined, the thinking practice of the champion of radical autonomy must posit itself as an essentially non-pre-determined, unceasing creator of form out of the formlessness of the Chaos, the Groundless temporality. It is therefore a thinking that from the outset points, not to the closure or termination of historical becoming, but to its unceasing self-alteration in and through the awareness that accepts the Groundlessness *for what it is.*

Let us grant with Castoriadis that awareness of the Groundlessness of society and of the world underpins radical autonomous thinking. What then does this relationship to the Groundless involve? Castoriadis' discussion of the relationship of heteronomous subjectivity to the Groundless provides the basis for an answer by way of contrast. We noted above that historically, humanity has been unable to accept the Groundless for what it is, absolute alterity. For Castoriadis, it is this inability that explains the so-called 'need for religion'.[116] In providing a name for the unnameable and designating a place for it, 'religion realizes and satisfies both the experience of the Abyss and the refusal to accept it'. If religion is 'par excellence, the presentation/occultation of the Chaos'[117] then that which distinguishes the champion of radical autonomy must be the very deployment of alterity, as distinct from merely reporting on this possibility. For Castoriadis, the experience of otherness which subverts the disciplined, static and comforting stance of the subject who is fearful of accepting the Groundless, comes with *willing* the project of autonomy. When, as we observed above, Castoriadis invokes a primordial state of radical willing to explain the 'thoughtful doing and political thinking' aimed at the supersession of heteronomy, he is also proposing a solution to the question of the relationship between

---

116. Cornelius Castoriadis, *World in Fragments*, p. 324.

117. Cornelius Castoriadis, *World in Fragments*, p. 324.

thinking and being. Being becomes *explicitly* an unceasing becoming or 'to-be' when the subject knows they are and can become autonomous through the autonomous practice of the collective. In this case autonomous thinking is more than a quality that human beings possess; it characterizes the human *mode of being as a collective*. It follows that, given the Groundlessness of the human psyche, society and the world, radical willing understood as the willing singularity of the champion of radical autonomy must play a crucial role in activating the visionary practice of autonomy.

Radical autonomous willing characterizes the collective of individuals who experience their subjectivity as the place from which to enact a partial rupture of heteronomous society or, in other words, a shift in social-historical horizons from heteronomous to autonomous instituting. It is therefore also the place of social-historical time as the time of creation. Now if indeed heteronomous society and subjectivity implode precisely when in the thinking/willing of the champion of autonomy the subject's singularity meets the Groundless and becomes the radical time of an (in principle) achieved destruction and an (in principle) achievable creation, then such an encounter with the Groundless should not only make it possible for the autonomous subject to emerge as alone with their being in the sense of making their own time free from the heteronomy and existential comfort that come with covering over the Chaos of society and world. Instead, such an encounter should also make it possible for the autonomous subject *to present as significant* over and above creating/destroying significations. In other words, the awareness of the Groundlessness of the world and of society must somehow make it possible for the subject to emerge as *both* singular and significant. The autonomous subject must be capable of creating *recognizably* significant time given their relationship to the project of autonomy, a project that on Castoriadis' account, is universally significant. The project of autonomy is alive, permeated by the freedom of a perpetual creation/destruction, and universal when the participants in an autonomous collective,

of those who recognize each other as such, will their autonomous practice incessantly. Autonomous subjectivity must
be in a position to present as significant in the appropriate
way when it is imbued with the will that wills the project of
autonomy in such terms. But then exposure to the Chaos
must give rise, not only to the incessant creation of significations, but also to the incessant activation of significant
singularity.

If the above observations are correct, Castoriadis's concepts should be able to yield an account of the sort of relationship to significance we have just sketched, especially since
the champion of radical autonomy also assumes a place from
which to challenge the dominant significations operating in
the current neo-liberal public spaces. Castoriadis needs an
account of the power to bring together the significance characteristic of the project of autonomy with the very subjects
whose distinctive significance stems from their willing implication in this project or, in other words, he needs an account of the power of the political agent *to present as significant* while being situated in the heteronomous society he
seeks to transform.

AUTONOMOUS VERSUS HETERONOMOUS/
RELIGIOUS SIGNIFICANCE

As we noted above, Castoriadis' work offers an account of
what it means for the autonomous subject to present as significant largely by way of contrast with the heteronomy of a
broadly defined religious orientation. Castoriadis suggests
that heteronomous society's 'misrecognition [...] of its own
being as creation and creativity'[118] comes with 'the signification of signification'.[119] This latter is the idea that religion
supplies a paradigmatic answer to the question of the origin, cause, foundation or end of signification, a question
that arises for human beings given that the world is of itself

---

118. Cornelius Castoriadis, *World in Fragments*, p. 327.
119. Cornelius Castoriadis, *World in Fragments*, p. 314.

'senseless, devoid of signification'.[120] We have been using the term 'significance' to distinguish the question of the origin or foundation of signification from significatory practices in general. For Castoriadis this difference explains the profound connection between religion and the heteronomy of society: heteronomous society demands an account of its origins which religion supplies in terms of something extra-social.[121] Both religion and the heteronomous institution of society:

> aim at giving *one and the same* signification to being, to the world *and* to society. They *have to* mask the Chaos and in particular the Chaos that is society itself. They mask it in falsely recognizing it, through its presentation/occultation in furnishing it with an Image, a Figure, a Simulacrum.[122]

In explaining being, the world and society in terms of the form of the Sacred, religion responds to the question of the signification of signification with a sort of compromise. Although it recognizes that society is not reducible to '*what it is*, that society's 'real', 'empirical' existence does not exhaust it', it also 'denies the radical imaginary and puts in its place a particular imaginary creation, a signification that comes to society from elsewhere'.[123] In the light of the above, we can contrast the aloneness of autonomous singularity, which refuses to cover over the Chaos, with what we might call the loneliness of religious singularity, which is made significant by appeal to a (loving) God. Whereas the former presents as creating significance through its own willing, the latter denies its creativity in misrepresenting itself as receiving significance from an extra-social source.

On the face of it, elucidating the significant singularity of the radical autonomous subject largely by way of contrast with the believer might seem misplaced given that heteronomous societies are not coextensive with religious societies. Indeed, one might argue that in championing radical

120. Cornelius Castoriadis, *The Castoriadis Reader*, p. 363.

121. Cornelius Castoriadis, *World in Fragments*, p. 318.

122. Cornelius Castoriadis, *World in Fragments*, pp. 319–320.

123. Cornelius Castoriadis, *World in Fragments*, pp. 325–326.

autonomy Castoriadis is already invoking the post-religious horizon of western liberal societies. In such case the relevant point of comparison would need to be, not so much the (society of the) believer, but (the society of) those who share with Castoriadis a secular orientation consistent with the times. After all, the effectiveness of Castoriadis' intervention depends upon its potential to create a partial rupture within the current institution of society. Nonetheless, for Castoriadis an explicitly secular heteronomous society is *not* non-religious in the relevant sense. Here it is worth noting that he takes religion, or more precisely the religious drive, to *organize* heteronomous society.[124] Indeed every heteronomous society has been essentially religious, according to Castoriadis, because:

> in situating the origin of the institution obligatorily in the same place as its own origin—external to society—religion has always been the central expression, essential vehicle, and ultimate guarantor of the heteronomy of society.[125]

He thus suggests that the core of religion—its insistence on identifying being with signification and denying that the world as such is always 'something more'—also characterizes modern western secular societies. In other words, a quasi-religious dimension persists here too given that the origin and operation of being, the world and society are similarly 'tied together', albeit in and through 'rationality', 'the laws of nature' or 'the laws of history'.[126] Accordingly, those who endorse a teleological view of history, or the wisdom and destiny of the revolutionary party, or who affirm various anthropological givens, or, in other words, those who affirm any secular version of heteronomy, which nonetheless satisfies our incredibly compromising *need to believe* and which seeks salvation in absolutes much like the religious version, present another point of contrast with the mode of being of autonomous singularity which is not

---

124. Cornelius Castoriadis, *World in Fragments*, pp. 318–319.
125. Cornelius Castoriadis, *The Castoriadis Reader*, p. 329.
126. Cornelius Castoriadis, *World in Fragments*, p. 318.

fundamentally dissimilar to the believer.[127]

It follows that Castoriadis attributes the radical willing that informs the visionary practice of autonomy to the mode of being of those who are liberated from *both* the religious and the quasi-religious orientations just described. The significance characterizing the autonomous subject's self-presentation should therefore not be confused either with the signification of signification that religion supplies or with any variation upon this that similarly appeals to an extra-social ground to explain the origin or nature of society. Let us refer to all such appeals as invoking the 'heteronomy of significance'. In order for the subject to present as recognizably significant, then the truly radical encounter with the Groundless must have the kenotic (emptying) power to purify the will and disassociate it from all the varieties of signification informing the heteronomy of significance.

FROM THE HETERONOMY OF SIGNIFICANCE TO THE HETERONOMY OF INSIGNIFICANCE

We can agree that Castoriadis's attempt to elucidate the autonomy of significance by juxtaposing the heteronomy of significance points in the direction of an account of the connection between the significance informing the project of autonomy with that of a willing singularity who identifies with this project. Nonetheless, such an account will remain incomplete in so far as it fails to provide a way of distinguishing the autonomy of significance from heteronomous

127. Stathis Gourgouris explains heteronomous societies' historical deferral to external authorities in terms of a process of self-occultation of the self-altering force emerging with the (social) subject's internalization of power, a process that he analyses as analogous with the internalization of alterity enacted by the human psyche (Stathis Gourgouris, 'Autonomy and Self-alteration', pp. 263-264). While it is clear that the force of subjection pertains to the social imaginary institution of society and not only to the radical imagination of the human psyche, it remains unclear why the processes of self-alteration and, hence, of self-occultation, should be considered symmetrical in the way Gourgouris' discussion implies.

activity that is not reducible to the heteronomy of signifi-cance. To develop this argument, we must complicate Castoriadis's treatment of contemporary heteronomous neo-liberal subjectivity. Let us imagine the case of a willing singularity who, despite appearing to share the qualities that the champion of autonomy attributes to the visionary prac-tice of autonomy, nonetheless stops short of activating this practice. Is it possible for the subject who refuses to *receive* significance, in the way the believer's significance is exter-nally derived, to face the Groundlessness of society and the world, and yet posit their singularity in terms *other than* sig-nificance? Might such a subject present as *insignificant,* in the sense of affirming and perpetuating what already is, and so remain heteronomous? Let us call this possibility of af-firming insignificance while facing the Chaos 'the heteron-omy of insignificance'.

One might think that this notion of 'the heteron-omy of insignificance' is conceptually impossible within Castoriadis' theoretical framework since affirming oneself in the very act of explicitly exposing the Groundless is a power that Castoriadis attributes exclusively to the autono-mous creator of new *eidos*. However, as we have seen, for Castoriadis autonomous subjectivity is available as a genu-ine alternative to heteronomous modes of social being, in so far as they differ at the ontological level. In other words, Castoriadis takes autonomous and heteronomous subjectiv-ity to be marked by a fundamental difference in orientation towards the Chaos. Accordingly, the mode of being of radi-cal democratic subjectivity can and must be distinguished by the appropriate response to the Chaos of society and the world. From this perspective the fundamental difference between autonomous and heteronomous conceptions of democratic subjectivity lies in their responses to the Chaos: whereas consumerist conceptions misrepresent or refuse to recognize the Chaos for what it is, autonomous subjects 'ac-cept the Chaos as Chaos'.[128]

Moreover, Castoriadis cannot merely assume that every

---

128. Cornelius Castoriadis, *World in Fragments*, p. 324.

mode of heteronomous activity is reducible to the heteronomy of religious significance. Even though acceptance of the Groundless is the precondition for the activation of the visionary practice of autonomy, it does seem that in order to interpret something like the Christian God as a supreme expression of the master signification of transcendence that has exhausted its meaning-generating potential, one must have already taken a step towards facing the Groundless and, to this extent, one no longer relies upon the comforting filtering of the Groundless. If this is correct, and bearing in mind his critique of quasi-religious orientations, we ought to demand of Castoriadis's conceptual framework that it make sense of a subjectivity defined in terms of the heteronomy of insignificance, one that is irreducible to the heteronomy of significance. We therefore ask: 'under what conditions and for whom might activity that embraces the Chaos nonetheless give rise to the heteronomy of insignificance?' To address this question, we return to Castoriadis' comments on the insignificance characterizing contemporary modern western societies and their inhabitants.

As we observed in Chapter 2, Castoriadis acknowledges the hold of insignificance on the current times, of the devaluation of everything as a result of consumerism and political apathy. Although he intends this as an empirical observation, in suggesting that everything, the totality of our world, radiates in the direction of producing an all-encompassing insignificance, he also implicitly allows for the possibility that insignificance is more than an incidental or occasional by-product of the heteronomy of western neo-liberal capitalism. It may also characterize the *mode of being* of the social thus instituted. In such a case those who would open themselves to the current social-historical conditions *as insignificant* manifest insignificance as their mode of being. As we suggested in the previous chapter, the point is not to examine the effects of some loss of the power of radical imagination but rather to make sense of a willing (mis)direction of this power towards a perpetuation of what Castoriadis would consider heteronomous norms and ways and, moreover, to

enact such a process through the exercise of the sorts of critical reflective powers that otherwise position modern subjects to take up the project of autonomy. What would this en-
tail in practice? In order to address this question, we must
establish the relationship of the abovementioned consumerist, politically apathetic subjectivity to the historically gener-
alised enactment of what we may call 'modern western proprietary being'. In the next chapter we will elaborate this
notion in greater detail. For present purposes 'proprietary
being' refers to modern practices that centre person-thing
relations in ways that enable subjects to present as formally universal through processes of abstracting from specificities of personal significance. In Castoriadian terms, in
observing this connection between proprietary being and
pseudo-democratic subjectivity within current conditions
we have a shift in focus from the heteronomous *instituted*
to the *instituting* practices of *heteronomous willing subjectivity*. As a mode of being of willing subjects proprietary being unavoidably implicates the subject in the insignificance
of the times since property-owning subjects are in principle
replaceable, and so denied the opportunity publicly to present as significant or, in other words, their social doing renders as private the subject's power to present singular being
as significant. For reasons that we examine in more detail
in Chapter 4, this orientation of proprietary being frees up
the power of a willing subject to encounter the Chaos of
the world in terms of indifference, a characterization that,
as we will see, Castoriadis also attributes to the Chaos. The
point we want to make here is that in so far as the indifferent world mediates the subject's owning relationships, the
exchange practices build on such relationships affirm the
Chaos of the world. And yet, proprietary exchange does not
give rise to ontological creation of *eidos* in the way this is en-
visaged for the visionary practice of autonomy. Instead, in
neo-liberal practices of *celebrating insignificance* owning and
exchange relations manifest modern capitalist heteronomy.
Castoriadis owes us an explanation for why it is not the case
that the current societal insignificance he acknowledges

does not also unavoidably implicate everyone through our involvement in this celebration of insignificance.

The above brief outline of the activity that exemplifies heteronomous insignificance suffices to demonstrate that the heteronomy of insignificance is not reducible to the heteronomy of significance that Castoriadis acknowledges. If our observations are sound, then the champion of radical autonomy must ultimately make effective the distinction between the autonomous subject's presentation as significant and the heteronomy of insignificance. That is, the relevant contrast becomes that between two modes of willing singularity, significant and insignificant, neither of which is captured by the heteronomy of significance that the believer exemplifies. From a perspective that takes the appropriate comparison to be that between the autonomy of significance and the heteronomy of insignificance, acknowledging that the corresponding singularities of these two modes of being similarly engage in exposing the Groundlessness of the world gives rise to a critical question: 'what remains to distinguish them in practice?'. In so far as Castoriadis is not able to answer this question, at least in terms of the analysis of an acceptance of the Groundlessness of the world if not of society, his elucidation of the radical potential of the subject's willing acceptance of the Groundless remains incomplete.

CONCLUSION

So far, in this and the previous chapter, our argument has been that Castoriadis is in a position to defend his conception of radical democratic subjectivity against the sort of concerns that contemporary thinkers such as Badiou and Brown raise against democratic practices only in so far as he can effectively distinguish the orientation of radical democratic subjectivity from the late twentieth century consumerist conceptions they critique. For this he must rely on an account, not only of the radical willing of singular subjects, but also of the autonomous collective's distinctive response to the Chaos. An account of the ontology of radical democratic subjectivity as a matter of exposing the Chaos of the world is therefore crucial for Castoriadis's theory. But is this deference to the Chaos adequate? In the next Chapter, we will begin to develop our claim that Castoriadis's account fails to convince. As we suggested at the outset, our argument is that exposing the Chaos cannot serve to distinguish Castoriadis's radical democratic citizen if this relationship to the Chaos is also a feature of the more widely shared practices that reproduce modern proprietary being. To explain how the reproduction of proprietary being constitutes activity that *exposes the Chaos of the world* in Castoriadis's sense, in the next chapter we offer a reading of the development of western subjectivity in the modern world, drawing on Hegel's discussion of the mode of being of abstract subjectivity. The aim will be not to assess Castoriadis by comparison with Hegel, but to lend plausibility to the claim that, in intervening reflectively in the process of their becoming, willing subjects may confront the Chaos yet not thereby activate their radical imagination towards autonomous political agency.

4. DEMOCRATIC SUBJECTIVITY:
A HEGELIAN RESPONSE

> To start from the self, to live in the self, [...] abstract
> subjectivity, when it is still empty, or rather has
> made itself to be empty; such is pure formalism, the
> abstract principle of the modern world.[129]

Castoriadis rejects the interpretive power of Hegel's claim
that beginning with the Roman Empire the modern world
has given rise to a mode of abstract being, a subjectivity currently formed as an 'empty' self. Yet his denial of the rele-
vance of this Hegelian idea to our times is too hasty. It is
based on the view that such ideas are the product of thinking that does not appropriately situate itself within the field
of the social-historical. The individual is after all socially fabricated, the product of an irreducible tension that exists between the social historical anonymous collective and the singular dimension of the human being rooted in the psyche.[130]
The experience of autonomous activity does not require any
emptying of the self since from Castoriadis's perspective to
think and act autonomously is to remain fully embedded in
concrete specificities; it is to experience genuine alterity or
otherness and 'otherness is always the otherness of *something* in respect to another *something*'.[131]

129. GWF Hegel, *Philosophy of History*, trans. J Sibree, New York, Dover
Publications, 1956, pp. 316-317.

130. Cornelius Castoriadis, *World in Fragments*, p. 143.

131. Cornelius Castoriadis, *World in Fragments*, p. 394, emphasis added.

Let us observe, firstly, that in liberal capitalist societies modern western subjectivity has been disassociated from any immediate (unreflective) connections to substantive universal values. That is, in our public lives we are systematically discouraged from invoking richly filled values that we treat as universal without having to justify their status as such. Whereas pre-modern western social contexts and discourses conflate particular ethical values with the universal, a universal that in turn functions as a kind of (natural) given, modern subjects are called upon, not only to adopt values through critical reflection, but also to question their universal application, as Castoriadis himself points out. The purported universality of claims that we might otherwise have taken for granted is itself exposed to the possibility of rigorous critical scrutiny. This much is consistent with Castoriadis's interpretation of the emergence of a new mode of human being in western modernity, the reflective and deliberating subjectivity discussed in the previous chapters.

Secondly, Castoriadis would agree as well that outside our designated private spaces, we are called upon always to speak from our positions as *particular* individuals or collectives, as particular embodiments of this or that way of being and doing. So, for example, in liberal capitalist societies our world-view, like our way of life and our vision of the good, comes to be understood as the personal, spiritual and ethical convictions of an individual or of a member of a social group in their capacity as a particular unit of agency. Liberal discourse registers precisely this kind of affirmation of our particular being with its insistence on locating substantive ethical and spiritual values in the domain of the private or non-public sphere. This is the legacy of recognizing the so-called 'fact of reasonable pluralism', the acknowledgement that, even after full argument and debate, reasonable people will still disagree about the nature of the good and how we might come to an appreciation of it.[132]

Thirdly, we also agree with Castoriadis that modern subjects are no longer assumed to be the bearers of universal

132. John Rawls, *Political Liberalism*, Columbia University Press, 1993.

values that are received from the outside, so to speak, whether from our god(s) or our community, but have instead become self-identified sources of value. Even when we decide
that certain values are objective and universal, it is still up
to us as particular individuals freely to make these kinds
of judgements. So, the bearers of multiple, conflicting and
even incommensurable values inhabit modern western societies as an outcome, not just of the co-presence and interac-
tion of different world views, but also of the very character of
modern western subjectivity. In engaging in the critical reflective activity that Castoriadis endorses this character does
not remain unaffected.

Castoriadis does not realize the full implications of the
observation that in functioning as particular beings in the
negative sense of not immediately (unreflectively) identifying with universal values, modern western subjects' experience of this negative relation has decisively impacted upon
the mode of exercising their reflective powers. First, precisely because we can differentiate between our particular and
our universal being in the abovementioned way, we are in
a position reflectively *to abstract* from all specificities, that
is, to reject particular aspects of our being and to identify
with others. Castoriadis insists that we create, rather than
identify with, aspects of our particular being/becoming. As
he points out, in its most basic form the modern subject is
self-determining. But this also means that the being of the
subject that gives itself its particular determinations is not
reducible to (the sum of) these particulars. This in turn renders the self-determining power of modern western subjectivity as wholly abstract. This 'emptying' brings the self back
to its pure singularity, a singularity, expressed in the personal pronoun 'I', which grounds itself in its immediate self-centred awareness. Of course, for Castoriadis, this Hegelian account of the process of arriving at the pure immediacy of the
'I' as a result of abstracting from all specificities reflects the
inherited tradition's problematic tendency towards nostal-
gia for an impossible, unmediated simple origin.[133] But the

133. Here we distinguish between Castoriadis's account of the process of

self's immediate awareness, or pure self-concern, supplies *the form* of our being in western modernity in the sense that it constitutes us as *formally* free. This is the framework of possibilities within which we actively position ourselves in relation to specificities, such race, ethnicity, gender, class, sexuality, and so on. Accordingly, the subject's formal freedom is 'empty' in the sense of being conceived as lacking any pre-given substantial determinations whatsoever.

Second, and perhaps more importantly, quite apart from our subjective awareness, in liberal capitalist societies this abstract mode of being is institutionally inscribed. We invoke it whenever we function as citizens, as legal subjects or as participants in the now global market economy. This institutional reinforcement of our reflective power of abstraction has an important social-historical consequence for modern western subjectivity. It positions us to recognize both the independence of our abstract mode of being from its substantive contents and the fact that this independence in turn renders our being as formal. Following this recognition the continuity of our being depends upon a certain *form* whose multiple (potential) contents become endlessly variable. Currently in modernity our essential nature is thus the very formality that is made possible through a subjectively recognizable and institutionally reinforced exercise of the abovementioned power of abstraction. As formally free subjects who do not immediately identify with the universal, we conform to what we have elsewhere called 'the formal universality of particularity'. Taking particularity to be the

subjectivation and in particular his complex theory of the primal subject's monadic core and the ways this relates through radical imagination to a heterogeneous world, from our present discussion of the social-historical processes through which it is now open to the socially fabricated individual of the modern world to reflectively create distance from all specificities. For a classic enlightening discussion of the former and it implications for Habermas's famous critique of Castoriadis , see Joel Whitebook, 1989 'Intersubjectivity and the Monadic Core of the Psyche: Habermas and Castoriadis on the unconscious', *Praxis International*, No. 4, pp. 347-364. For a critique of Castoriadis's conception of the psyche's monadic core, arguing for a more 'plural' idea, see Karl E. Smith, *Meaning Subjectivity Society: Making Sense of Modernity*, Leiden and Boston, Brill, 2010, p. 111.

universal form of subjects who do not immediately identify with any substantive universal values, this principle supplies the form that constrains social being in today's world.[134]

The abovementioned recognition of particularity represents a shift of attention from what something is as a specific entity to how it is located in a network of particulars. It is significant for our purposes that we can understand this shift from the 'what' to the 'how' of modern western subjectivity via our Hegelian account of the enactment of proprietary being.[135] The power of property-owning plays a crucial role at the ontological level of our encounters in the global world because the idea of proprietary subjectivity defines the fundamental relationship between the subject in her capacity as a formal being and her world understood as the external manifestation of this being. For such proprietary being, everything beyond the subject's own abstract being has the potential to be transformed into a property item. Modern western subjects thus have the capacity to (mis)treat their nation, ethnicity, children, body, skills, talents, and so on, as private property. Here, our focus is on property-owning as a power or capacity of human beings, as distinct from moral and legal discourses of property ownership that presuppose this fundamental power.

One implication of the emptiness of formal subjectivity is that it makes the being of all particulars a matter of their accessibility to the property-owning subject. The modern western subject's abstract self-relation manifests the subject's very power to re-conceive and organise the world in a way that enables the subject to affirm itself in it. In other words, the world is already implicated in the subject's power of abstraction as the world of the subject, as the world that exists to serve the subject. The subject's activity of abstracting is, therefore, the point of potentiality out of which to create reality in conformity with the subject's self-centred

134. Toula Nicolacopoulos and George Vassilacopoulos, *Hegel and the Logical Structure of Love*, Melbourne, re.press, 2010, Part I and especially p. 35.

135. G W F Hegel, *Philosophy of Right*, trans. T M Knox, Oxford, Oxford University Press, 1981, §34–§104.

awareness. In this way, the subject's power of self-determination is formulated in terms of something to be achieved
rather than as a given. Unlike the epistemological awareness of the Cartesian subject that progressively leaves behind every specific aspect of the world in a (futile) effort to
achieve self-certainty, the Hegelian subject's awareness is
not trapped in its own internal space. It is constituted from
the outset as what we might call 'the will-to-be'. Hence, for
Hegel, the first imperative of the subject is: 'be as a person'.[136] At the same time, by implicating the world in its abstracting activity, the modern western subject makes manifest the fundamental terms of its potential being in the
world. From its position of a will-to-be, understood in the
above terms, the external world — everything beyond the
self-centred awareness of subjectivity — is constituted as its
immediate other in the dual sense of an irreducibly different
and separable other. From the position of the will-to-be, this
immediate other is constituted as that which exists without
a will of its own. This is what Hegel refers to as 'the thing'.
The Hegelian thing is a specificity, any particular whatsoever, that the subject positions as infinitely indifferent to itself
and, hence, as capable of limitlessly receiving a will from the

136. G W F Hegel, *Philosophy of Right*, §36. In the *Imaginary Institution
of Society*, pp. 105-106, Castoriadis explains the place of the other in
the structure of subjectivity via a critique of the Cartesian subject that
permeates 'traditional philosophy'. To explain this anti-Cartesian moment
in Castoriadis's account of psychic alterity Stathis Gourgouris draws on
Judith Butler's Hegelian inspired account of the formation of subjectivity
and, in particular, her discussion of the 'tropological inauguration of
the subject' whereby the formative power of subjectivity is 'marked by a
figure of [...] turning back upon itself or even a turning *on* oneself' at the
moment when 'there is no subject' to make such a turn, thereby rendering
'permanently uncertain' its own ontological status: Judith Butler cited in
Stathis Gourgouris, 'Autonomy as Self-Alteration', p. 258. In restricting
our discussion to the modern subject's capacity to enact a certain mode of
reflection, our reading and use of Hegel in the present context bypasses
this discussion and does not seek to challenge this analysis of the place
of alterity in the formation of the subject. Nor does it seek to reject
Castoriadis's critique of rational mastery in relation to the subject. On the
purposes of psychoanalysis in relation to this see Ojeili, 'Post-Marxism
with Substance', p. 236.

outside, so to speak. Such unrestricted receiving of a will is the very enactment of the thing's indifference. It is a thing that is in itself empty of will and, hence, something penetrable. This is why under appropriate conditions the subject positioned as the will-to-be can choose to inhabit the thing. Within this conceptual framework, the thing is just as much an abstraction as the category of the formally free subject. Their difference lies in the idea that the latter actively draws upon the former: the will that is empty of concrete being depends upon the being of an existent that is empty of will.

This construction of the world is currently indispensable to the ways in which modern western subjects function in the world, irrespective of whether we disapprove of this logic at an intellectual level. For example, as the will-to-be in the world, formally free subjects inevitably de-spiritualize the world of particulars. This enables the inhabitants of western modernity to relate to the thing in terms of embodying their own will in it, thereby transforming it into their own property. Wilful possession of what was previously a will-less thing constitutes a primary form of embodiment; it is invoked whenever we assert: 'this is mine'. That is, in becoming what I am through my own act of will, and without the direct involvement of another will, I achieve for myself a kind of grounding that enables me to relate securely to myself as a concrete being and to my particular place in the world. It is this kind of self-grounding that underpins modern western ideals of cosmopolitan lifestyles and consumerist orientations in the absence of a commitment to the universal orienting power of substantive values.[137]

The subject–world relation we have been describing also harbours a contradiction, given that every act of possession does in fact implicate another will. Indeed, embodiment of a will in a thing presupposes a certain form of recognition. In transforming the thing into my property, I extend myself into it and make it my concrete being, but within the framework generated by the logic of the abovementioned formal universality of particularity, property must be alienable.

137. See, for example, Irene Watson, 'First Nations'.

That is, it must be capable of being transferred to another property-owning subject. The maintenance of this sort of distance between the subject and its property items perpetuates the formalism inherent in our way of being. Without the alienability of property, which protects proprietary being from becoming locked into the concrete particularity of the property item, our formal freedom would be compromised. So, the mutual recognition of property-owners is an indispensable feature of our social interactions. Indeed, modern western subjects encounter others as subjects by recognizing them as private property-owning. Because exchange relations manifest this fundamental form of mutual recognition, their ongoing re-enactment plays the role of affirming this dominant way of being in western modernity, just as custom and religion might do in different socio-historical contexts. In our secularized world that has broken ties with an authoritative tradition, the recognition of formal subject-to-subject relations relies on the idea of the will-less thing instead. This is why we become complicit in consumer society and continue to be drawn into the global network of commodity circulation, even when we are convinced by social critiques of western modernity, of its notions of formal freedom and of our related environmental abuses and injustices to non-western peoples.

On the Hegelian account we have just sketched, the enactment of abstract, property-owning subjectivity presupposes the *indifference* of the world. Here, 'the world' refers to nature understood as the radical other of subjects as singular units of self-concern. Indeed, the practice of owning something specific exposes the mode of being or universality of this indifference. We suggested above that the practice of owning redirects us from the 'what' to the 'how' of property-owning ontology. It also involves a parallel shift from the 'what' of the thing owned to its mode of being. Irrespective of their substantive differences, that things, for example, this land or these trees, are owned presupposes that they are radically equal in relation to the capacity to be owned. In other words, that they are owned presupposes that they equally belong to the set of things constituting potential property items, and which, prior to actually being owned, may nonetheless be identified as such by the subject capable of acting as a property owner. The subject must be capable of making the realm of ownability or, the mode of being of indifference, accessible. This realm of the ownable is the horizon in which the subject positions itself to enact their self-concern, the will-to-be, through the practice of owning things. Prior to actually owning this or that specific thing, the owning subject becomes the bearer of such horizon in gathering together all things, present and future, as well as any combination of these, as ownable.

In this way the subject posits itself as the bearer of the world's indifference, the universal mode of being of the world, in which things in general are positioned so as to reveal their capacity to embody the subject's willing being. We have suggested that the infinite penetrability of the thing enables the infinite realizability of the will-to-be. The will-to-be is intentional towards specific things at the same time as directing itself away from things and towards itself as the agent who, in exercising self-concern, wills their willing. This will-to-will is the infinite element in self-concern and the ultimate source of the formal subject's significant agency. It is at this level of *willing* the will-to-be that subjects affirm their atomic being and the drive to externalize it. So, by implicating the world's mode of being, its indifference, in this process, the subject posits himself/herself as exclusively self-concerned. Owning, or the enactment of the will-to-be, is the act through which the thing owned is 'abstracted' from its whatness in order for its mode being to be affirmed as indifferent. Owning 'elevates' the specific thing owned to the universal horizon of indifference and at the same time draws this horizon down to the thing, so to speak, which embodies this indifference. It follows that owning has a cosmic dimension and the practice of owning has the potential to reveal the cosmic aloneness of self-concerned beings, the fact that we are alone in a world that is indifferent both to us and to its own being.[138]

Castoriadis recognizes and invokes the indifference of the world when he tries to explain why the world depends upon the Chaos. But if humanity is truly alone in the cosmos so that its significations derive exclusively from its own self-relating in the way that Castoriadis maintains, of itself the world must be *absolutely* indifferent, that is, indifferent to signification *as such* and not just to this or that set of social imaginary significations. Castoriadis confirms this when attempting to explain the very possibility of the heterogeneity of social imaginary significations throughout history:

> In relation to imaginary time, as well as to the whole edifice of imaginary significations erected by each society, we ask: How must the world be, in itself, in order that this amazing and unlimited variety of imaginary edifices can be erected? The only possible answer is: The world must be tolerant and indifferent as between all these creations. It must make room for them, and for all of them, and not prevent, favour, or impose any among them over and against the others. In short: the world must be void of meaning. It is only because there is no signification intrinsic to the world that humans had, and were able, to endow it with this extraordinary variety of strongly heterogeneous meanings.[139]

Here Castoriadis draws our attention to the *indifference* of the world to signification in order to explain the rich variety of social imaginary significations the theorist encounters when examining responses to the Groundlessness of the world across different societies and times. Viewed diachronically we appreciate the contingency characterizing the panorama of social-historical formations, which have come into being largely unaware of their ontological horizon

138. We could mention here in passing that the radicalization of revealing the indifference of the world that we refer to as nature through the general and radical practice of owning that is liberated from constraints of tradition, religion, etc, is the fundamental presupposition for the mathematical knowing of nature. Scientific knowing is grounded on owning as the power to expose indifference as the mode of being of nature.

139. Cornelius Castoriadis, *World in Fragments*, p. 389.

of indifference that they mostly cover up, as Castoriadis is at pains to explain. But we can also appreciate the same point in relation to the synchronic generation of social imaginary significations within any particular society. That is, if the world must be indifferent in order for us to make sense of 'the whole edifice of imaginary significations erected by each society', it must be no less so in relation to the unlimited variety of significations that are created *within* any particular society. The above observation—that the world makes room for synchronic plurality of significations within a particular society and not just across history and societies—entails that the world's indifference opens a space for the unlimited proliferation of meaning-generating choices and commitments of the sort we encounter in modern western liberal capitalism, a proliferation that, in turn, renders explicit the unlimited plurality of significations *in their particularity*. When viewed synchronically within the horizon of a specific society, every specific value created must presumably take its place in the society regardless of the degree of its significance. It follows that the willing participants of such a pluralist society are in a position, not merely to embrace the substantive content of whatever they happen to present as significant, but also to recognize the mode of being of that which is re(presented) within the terms of the formal universality of particularity, that is as *one particular amongst the plurality of particulars* or, conversely, as a particular that is *not immediately identified with the universal*.

Castoriadis's theory is compatible with our claim that the mode of being of willing subjects conforms to the formal universality of particularity. In his terms, we can say that subjects who are aware of their mode of being as such do not derive their significance from, or attribute the source of signification to, an external source. But in advancing the claim that the world is indifferent, Castoriadis also suggests that the fully enlightened subject is able to engage directly with this indifference, even though this is not typically the case for heteronomous society. For, the visionary practice of autonomy entails facing the Chaos of the world and the world's indifference to any and all signification. Accordingly, if as participants in a pluralist society, we primarily encounter each other in the field of the formal universality of particularity and this encounter is mediated by our acknowledgement of the indifference of the world, then it seems appropriate to ask how else this subject-relationship might be enacted.

This said, in the above cited passage Castoriadis appears to be simply inferring the world's indifference as a matter of empirical observation regarding the historical plurality of meanings. Nonetheless, if they are to be effectively distinguished, that is, distinguished *in their practice*, Castoriadis's autonomous radical democratic subjects—those who he suggests expose the Chaos of the world with their activity—must be shown to be (capable of) acting in a way that exposes the world's absolute indifference. They must be shown to confront the world's indifference directly in their experience of the world since it is this experience, rather than an intellectual relationship, that is at stake in the differentiation of the orientation of the autonomous collective of radical democratic subjects from the pseudo-democrats that Castoriadis critiques. But when we turn from the 'what' to the 'how' of the property-owning practice we find that the enactment of property-owning relations already exposes the world's cosmic indifference, albeit through the singular subject's relationship to the thing and to exchange. In liberal capitalist societies radicals and pseudo-democrats alike are already implicated in the practice of owning in their shared capacity as modern western subjects. This is why exposing the Chaos of the world cannot possibly *distinguish* the radical democratic subject.

RADICAL DEMOCRATIC SUBJECTIVITY AND THE EMPTY SUBJECT OF THE MODERN WORLD

We suggested above that in liberal capitalism the enactment of proprietary being that exposes the indifference of the world also manifests the *universal form* of willing subjectivity in so far it involves a singular subject who wills its will-to-be. If we are right about this, then despite Castoriadis's own failure to make this connection with the radical willing of democratic subjects that he invokes, we should expect his account of willing subjectivity to remain within the restrictive parameters of this universal form. To put the same point differently, we should be able to indicate how modern western property-owning subjects are in a position, either to affirm the institutions and consumerist practices of the global liberal capitalist order, what we referred to in Chapter 3 as exemplifying the heteronomy of insignificance, or to turn against these practices precisely because and in so far as they ground their being as subjects in the empty formalism that characterizes their willing activity. The subject's willing activity is so emptily plastic that it can endlessly give itself opposing forms, thus creating a vicious spiral, which sinks into the depths of its formalism so much so that it has no hope of escape, even when, like Castoriadis, one seeks to overcome that which one considers politically unacceptable. According to Hegel,

> [...] this unrestricted possibility of abstraction from every determinate state of mind which I may find in myself or which I may have set up in myself [...] When the will's self-determination consists in this alone or when representative thinking regards this side [of the will] by itself as freedom and clings fast to it then we have negative freedom [...] This is the freedom of the void which rises to a passion and takes shape in the world; [...] when it turns to actual practice, it takes shape in religion and politics alike as the fanaticism of destruction—[...] Only in destroying something does this negative will possess the feeling of itself as existent. Of course, it imagines that it is willing some positive state of affairs, such as universal equality or universal religious life.[140]

Our interest is not to compare Hegel and Castoriadis's claims regarding the void in connection with the human psyche.[141]

140. GWF Hegel, *The Philosophy of Right*, §5, Remark.

141. For a general discussion of Castoriadis's theory of the abyssal psyche see Chamsy Ojeili, 'Post-Marxism with Substance'.

Instead, here we want to highlight Hegel's focus on the way in which the 'freedom of the void' takes shape specifically in religious and political activity. Bearing in mind our discussion of Castoriadis so far, we can also draw upon these comments to assist us in identifying a certain correspondence between the currently available concrete shapes of willing subjectivity—the concrete forms of willing available to abstract subjects in Hegel's sense—and the Castoriadian categories of the instituting, the instituted and the institutable. In line with these categories we suggest that in so far as subjects enact their abstract, proprietary being within liberal capitalist society, three concrete forms of willing relationship to the (Chaos of the) world become available to them. Although Hegel does not refer to it in the above cited passage, the first of these three forms involves an affirmation of the existing order. In this case the subject is constituted through their willing implication in the very 'circulation of desires' and 'short-run gratifications' that, as we saw in Chapter 2, Badiou and Brown respectively assign to the contemporary democratic subject. In affirming the instituted world of capitalism through such willing, the (heteronomous) mode of willing that characterizes consumerist conceptions of democratic subjectivity effectively *privileges the instituted*. Such privileging is entailed by the fact that liberal capitalism presupposes what we can call 'the privatization of significance', which goes hand in hand with the socially reinforced heteronomy of insignificance. It is because the willing subject attributes significance to its atomic subjective being that the most fundamental public significations embodied in liberal institutions are understood as value-free or neutral. The privatization of significance liberates the public realm of instituted significations in a way that makes it possible for them to delineate the social spaces for the co-existence of a plurality of value orientations that private citizens make significant.

What of the forms of willing that are given effect with the destructive religious and political activity that Hegel describes above? Both these forms involve the aspiration to break out of the current mode of instituted society. As we noted above, these possibilities arise because, as the power to privatize significance the willing subject is in a position to reject the current mode of instituted society, to see it as insignificant and seek alternative sources of significance. Let us consider these in turn.

First, in deferring to an extra-social instituting authority in God, the mode of willing that characterizes religion *privileges human beings as institutable*. In other words, this view gives primacy to the potential of the anonymous collective to receive its God-given shape, the community of believers. As we saw in Chapters 2 and 3, Castoriadis advocates a form of willing that presents as an alternative to both the consumerist and religious forms of willing and in the latter case it is the problematic misrepresentation of the source of signification to which he objects. Even so, his formulation of the relationship of the categories of the instituted, the instituting and the institutable is sufficiently broad to accommodate religious willing activity such as that which Oliver Davis describes in the following passage:

> [...] our self-knowing is simultaneously a recognition or condition of our unity. We do not mean by this some sense of self, which is transcendentally located outside history and the multiple narratives, which constitute our social and historical identity. [...] But we do wish to argue for a self who comes to itself precisely within such narratives, and within its relation with multiple forms of otherness. This is to affirm the self in its unity, as that which enables us to identify all the narratives of experience as existence that is 'mine'. Such a sense of unity is the ground of the narrative structure of experience as such, and also entails the recognition that something remains over from the dispersal of the self through the multiplication of its narratives, which is the 'metanarrativity' or 'essential narrativity' of the self. The historical thematization of this transcendence is as inwardness and interiority, which [...] signifies the sphere of pure self-possession transcendentally given within experience and resistant to reduction to history. This is the site

of our self-knowing as creature, and is the simultaneous recognition of our dependence on God in sinfulness, finitude and pride.[142]

For Davis religious subjectivity is thus conceived as rooted in the social-historical and defined by the 'multiple forms of otherness' that constitute its relations. Here, however, there is some scope for acknowledging society's self-instituting power and, hence, for taking up the task of destroying capitalism's institutions of domination, once the exteriority of the subject's being has been differentiated from its interiority so that God comes to inform the latter. In relation to the former, however, one can reasonably suggest that the experience of 'finitude', which amounts to a recognition of the insignificance of the singular as the private source of significance, is grounded in the ability of the singular to expose the indifference of the world via enactment of the generalized practice of owning, as we discussed above. But in this case, the singular can be said to seek significance—meaningfulness, as distinct from signification(s)—through the sacred. Hence the adoption of a form of willing that privileges the institutable, that is, the capacity of believers to form communality through their prior receiving of God's love. It follows that in rejecting today's politically apathetic consumer driven society one may well merely be masking the Chaos through deferral to an extra-social authority via the sacred, as Castoriadis insists. Nonetheless, for the purposes of our argument it is noteworthy that, like the consumerist's form of willing, the form of willing of the modern religious subject also conforms to the constraints of the 'empty' subject. Rather than defining religious subjectivity in terms of the practice of masking the Chaos in seeking God, Davis' nuanced account supports the view that the religious subject's form of willing may in fact expose the Chaos as the precondition for both the practice of privatizing significance and the rejection of this privatization.

The final form of willing we want to consider is that

---

142. Davis, David, O, A Theology of Compassion, Michigan, Cambridge, Eerdmans, 2003, pp. 8-9.

which underpins Castoriadis's radical democratic subject. Our claim is that radical democratic subjectivity is similarly implicated in the inwardness of the void that Hegel describes and thus illustrates a third form of willing that liberal capitalist society makes available. In seeking the radical creation and destruction of *nomos*, this third form of willing *privileges the instituting* power of the subject. Like religious subjectivity that privileges the institutable, radical democratic subjectivity aspires to create community, albeit in the shape of the democratic collective. But this aspiration is not linked to an external authority, like God. It derives instead from the radical democratic subject's own willing, which, like the religious subject, rejects the privatization of significance. At the same time, unlike the religious subject who seeks significance from the divine, Castoriadis's subject treats its own willing activity as the source of universal significance. In treating its self-concern and, therefore, the power of abstraction as the power to institute society, the radical subject posits *the willing subject as such* as the ultimate creator of significations. The willing subject is thus elevated to the bearer of the command to ceaselessly institute the collective and its institutions.

In Chapter 3 we saw that Castoriadis opens himself to the objection that he fails to assign a real place in his theory to significant social being in advocating the autonomy of significance only by way of contrast to the heteronomy of significance that he attributes to the prevailing (quasi)-religious attitude without considering the possibility of heteronomous *insignificance*. Paradoxically, it is in this gesture of rejecting God as the source of heteronomous significance that the radical democratic subject encounters the believer as the other side of the same act, that of abstracting from the communal. More specifically, we can detect the source of an unacknowledged abstraction in the radical democratic subject's activity of seeking the collective. This is an abstraction from the communal understood as the source of the significance of unconditional togetherness, the source of meaningfulness that is capable of transforming the insignificant

singular being who accepts the Chaos into a being with significance, or in other words, of transforming such singular
being into the bearer of the bond of universal communality. In comparing the link between tragedy and the political
in the work of Castoriadis and Kostas Papaioannou, Natalie
Karagiannis indirectly offers a description of this notion
while implicitly affirming its absence from Castoriadis's
thought. Communality as the unconditional togetherness
that permeates singular beings with significance appears to
be at the heart of the idea of the revolutionary mass, one of
the concepts that differentiates Papaioannou's thought from
Castoriadis's. As Karagiannis observes, for Papaioannou the
revolutionary mass transforms itself from 'a formless being'
to a meaningful Chorus as a precondition for becoming 'a
voting body that asks for just decisions'. The revolutionary
mass is 'that "being" which emerges every now and then
in history and has the potential to revolutionize the social
and political by deciding—or being convinced of—the future course of the polity'.[143]

Notice that for both Castoriadis's radical democrat and
Davis's religious subject the call to institute society is not
the call *of* community in the sense of the indeterminate,
uninstitutable community which when reflected upon and
experienced as the ultimate source of the significance of
belonging is not reducible to the mere result of a process.
Instead for both the call to institute is a call *to create* community, even though the source of this call differs and is
respectively the radical willing subject and the loving God.
Here the subject who seeks the communal is not the subject who draws significance from the being of the collective
itself, a being whose substance is not reducible to the singular subject's radical willing.[144] Rather, the willing sub-

143. Natalie Karagiannis, 'The Tragic and the Political: A Parallel
Reading of Kostas Papaioannou and Cornelius Castoriadis', *Critical
Horizons*, vol. 7, no. 1, 2006, pp. 303-319, at pp. 312-313.

144. As we noted Chapter 3, Andreas Kalyvas makes a similar point
about the irreducibility of the collective will to the singular will. However,
his point is in connection with Castoriadis's conception of democratic
decision-making procedures and not in relation to the idea of substantive

ject is the atomic subject who, being empty of community, seeks it at the same time as devaluing or exaggerating
its significance.[145] Castoriadis's reliance on a view of atomic subjectivity, in the abovementioned sense of disregarding
the place of non-reductive community, is evidenced in his
treatment of the autonomous collective, which, as we have
already observed, draws exclusively upon radical willing
subjects' shared knowing and doing. (Recall from Chapter 3
that the supersession of heteronomous society is possible in
so far as *each one of us wills* it and *knows that* others will it as
well, so that the autonomous collective is at best a group of
like-minded individuals.) By seeking the collective, the radical democratic subject does indeed oppose the privatization
of significance, but in doing so they merely find their own
'void', since aiming to create the autonomous collective presupposes a detachment of the socially fabricated individual from the community. The collective is reduced to *an aim
to be achieved* by otherwise dispersed individuals who know
nothing of the substantive power of the call of community ('gather as gathered') and of the experience of receiving
this call as their unconditional starting point for pursuing
the aim of exercising their instituting power. It follows that
with Castoriadis's abstraction from the call of community,
the modern western subject's formalism is here exposed in
its apotheosis as the instituting power of the *nomos*.

We have argued that in the light of its presupposed abstraction from the call of the uninstitutable or unwillable
community, formal subjectivity faces three potential paths
corresponding to the three forms of concrete willing: (1) the
otherwise insignificant subject may choose to accept their
insignificance (the consumerist democrat); (2) they may seek

communality.

145. Our reference here to the 'atomic subject' is not co-extensive with
the 'neoliberal subject' of Klimis's analysis, which we saw in Chapter
2, she identifies as a 'social *analoga*' to Castoriadis's understanding
of the psychic monad. While Klimis's general description of neo-
liberal subjectivity conforms to our Hegelian understanding of atomic
subjectivity, this latter draws on the structure of modern proprietary
being in the terms we outlined above.

significance through the sacred (the religious subject); or (3) the subject may seek significance in its own power of will-ing (Castoriadis's radical democratic subject). Each of these responses to the world of liberal capitalism conforms to the mode of being of empty subjects in Hegel's sense. With this in mind, we are now in a position to appreciate one of the implications of the emptiness or the void that is the core of proprietary being, the generalized mode of being character-izing empty subjects within western liberal societies. In so far as the reflective subject is empty of the orienting power of the communal, the substantive power of the uninstitu-table significance of the unwilling collective cannot inform the dimensions of the instituting, the institutable and the in-stituted that we mentioned at the outset. They therefore ap-pear as three disconnected dimensions of the Castoriadian (empty) subject's experience. Being oblivious to the primor-dial significance of the communal, the reflective subject can-not but view each of these three dimensions of experience as dispersed and externally related to one another and this in turn favours the privileging of one of them at the expense of the others. In the final section of this chapter we will il-lustrate the claim that Castoriadis privileges the instituting power of the subject in this way. Exemplifying Hegel's 'free-dom of the void', the radical democratic subject's instituting practice is made to depend upon an unceasing questioning that ultimately fails to question its own proper place.

QUESTIONING AND THE PRACTICE OF INSTITUTING

Drawing attention to Castoriadis' understanding of the dy-namism in socio-historical becoming, Sophie Klimis cites Castoriadis' reference to '"pulsating processes" in which phases of creation of forms alternate with phases of destruc-tion of forms' to explain Castoriadis' claim regarding the rhythmic, yet non-determined, movement of the 'true and genuinely singular' character of social-historical forms.[146]

146. Sophie Klimis, 'From Modernity to Neoliberalism', pp.144-145.

For Castoriadis, Klimis concludes:

> With 'rhythmicity', we do not speak of a combination of pre-existing and static elements, but of modulations that *are* the process of self-transforming of the socio-historical *eidos*. Therefore, talking about the rhythmicity of the *eidos* of modernity allows us to consider the question of its singularity, through the main *eidetic modulations* of Enlightenment, capitalism and neoliberalism.[147]

What we want to suggest here is that Castoriadis' appeal to the Chaos of the world ultimately betrays the need for a notion of the primordial communal gathering of radical subjects whose movement ultimately involves incessant transformation of the same *as new*. As we noted at the outset, according to Castoriadis's elucidation of the workings of a fully autonomous society, to affirm society's self-instituting power is not just to explicitly affirm the power to create new *nomos*, it is also to affirm *the power to incessantly question* what is created. For Castoriadis it is instructive that ancient Greece and modern Europe are the only times 'where questioning of the existing institutions has occurred'.[148] These two periods suggest the potential for a constant struggle between the autonomous self-reflective subjects who are the creators of their society's institutions and the institutions thus created, which serve to foster the forgetting of their social-historical making and in this struggle it is the practice of questioning that recalls the significance of 'social doing'. Let us explain.

For Castoriadis, the institution always has the tendency *to forget its origin* and to posit itself as an end in itself.[149] Radical questioning of society's norms is crucial for society's self-instituting because it is through such questioning that the radical instituting power safeguards against the ossification that the instituted is always in danger of producing, no matter how it is created. We might say that the institution tends to posit humanity as its *mere* receivers. Nonetheless, the integrity of the instituting activity of the autonomous

147. Sophie Klimis, 'From Modernity to Neoliberalism', p. 145.
148. Cornelius Castoriadis, 'The Greek Πόλις', p. 49.
149. Cornelius Castoriadis, *The Imaginary Institution*, p. 110.

collective requires that it not be absorbed in the instituted. Put differently, if it is to counteract the tendency of the institution to forget its origin, the power of instituting must always overflow the instituted. For this reason, despite opposing a purely proceduralist model of democracy (Chapter 2), ultimately what matters from the standpoint of Castoriadis's theory is the process of instituting *disassociated from* the product of such a process, that which is specifically instituted.[150] At the same time, Castoriadis does not credit the institution of itself with any (potential) significance. The significance of the institution derives from social doing, which as we observed in Chapter 3, characterizes radical politics aiming towards society's self-transforming. For both these reasons then—the disassociation of process from product and the assignment of only derivative significance to the product of creativity—Castoriadis's understanding of the workings of a fully autonomous society privileges the power and practice of instituting over the instituted.

Nonetheless, in Castoriadis's scheme, *the practice* of instituting effectively becomes reduced to the power of questioning. The distinguishing quality of the Castoriadian radical democratic subject becomes, not so much the will to create new *eidos* as Castoriadis maintains, but rather *the will to question* whatever has been created. After all, heteronomous societies also create their institutions and significations, albeit unknowingly. Recall that in highlighting the practice of questioning Castoriadis elucidates a process of re-capturing society's instituting power in order to avoid thinking of the instituted as fixed and instituted once and for all. However, this interest in preserving intact the power of instituting stems from an (implicit) abstraction from the communal, an abstraction that, as we noted above, grounds the privileging of the subject's formalism and reduces the

---

150. This is not to say that Castoriadis is not interested in making substantive judgements. As he comments in the context of a different discussion, 'I do not respect others' difference simply as difference and without regard to what they are and what they do.' Cornelius Castoriadis, *The Castoriadis Reader*, pp. 307-308. However, this does not affect the implications of this theory.

communal to an aim to be achieved. Since (perhaps due to his own political experience) Castoriadis does not conceive of the communal as unconditionally received and, hence, as the indeterminate and un-institutable source of significance, he does not take seriously the possibility of incorporating into his theory the idea of the perpetual (re)creation of the same institutions as the defining act of a genuinely autonomous society. In other words, his analysis loses sight of the ideas, firstly, that the creativity of radical democratic subjects presupposes their having, from the outset, the power of willing (through exercising their radical imagination) alongside self-concern as receivers of the primordial call of community; and, secondly, that the institutions they create are overflowed, not by the awareness of the instituting power of (the collective of) willing subjects, but by the significance of the indeterminate uninstitutable communal gathering. This unwilling overflowing, an overflowing that cannot be reduced to subjective willing, is the only power capable of perpetually resituating the members of the collective in their original position of receiving the call to (re)institute their society precisely because they are already situated as gathered in the significant field of togetherness. It is such overflowing that leads the institutions and the significations they embody back to the source of significance in a perpetual act of re-creating the same by recurrently experiencing it as new. In the absence of this sort of movement, namely the pulsating mutual informing of communal significance and the instituted significations that bring together the new and the same, the incessant practice of instituting can only be grounded on the activity of questioning. When the subject is not (re)posited as the creator of institutions they are not drawn back to the significant field of the communal and are thus not positioned to 'forget' the status of the already created thereby enabling the (re)activation of the process of creation as such. Here subjects have no other recourse but to remind themselves that they are the creator. But in this case, the already established institutions are the only reference point. Having been created, they must be actively re-membered *as-created* through incessant questioning. The practice of incessant questioning thus captures and re-activates the process of creating and it does so by prioritizing the power of questioning over the activity of creating/instituting as well as over that which is created. Creativity and creation are thus subordinated to the power of questioning.

When questioning is given primacy in this way, even though the possibilities for creation are multiple and remain open in accordance with the formal universality of particularity we discussed above, this openness remains true only of their content and not of their mode of being. On one level, as we have already suggested, whatever is created must inevitably conform to the formal universality of particularity. If the institution is created by the power of instituting and destroyed through the practice of questioning, every time an institution is created it must be taken to be a *particular* institution. But the privileging of the instituting over the instituted ultimately restricts the mode of being of the instituted in that it reduces it to the *destructible*. For as the guarantee against the ossifying tendency of institutions, the mode of being of whatever is created must conform to the potentially destructible. Since the fact of having been created is revealed in an institution's being destroyed, in principle, society's creativity becomes explicit with every act of destroying whatever has been created. Castoriadis thus relies on a kind of unacknowledged closure with respect to the mode of being of the instituted. This is why, even though the practice of incessant questioning provides the benefit of safeguarding the singularity of subjects— their singularity is not thereby absorbed by the institution— nevertheless, the privileging of incessant questioning in the way just described ultimately manifests the negativity that Hegel ascribes to the politically active empty subject.

CONCLUSION

If our argument is sound, Castoriadis's radical democratic subject is the apotheosis of the 'empty' self that Hegel identifies with the dominant mode of being in the modern world, namely the abstract being of proprietary subjectivity. In conforming thus to the possibilities available to this proprietary being, the power of instituting does not seem capable of taking us beyond the structures of global capitalism, despite Castoriadis's aspirations to the contrary. Castoriadis does not escape an inadvertent reduction of radical democratic subjectivity to the empty formalism that he otherwise opposes. His account of radical democratic subjectivity relies on a one-sided appreciation of the role that the Chaos, the Groundless or indifference of the world, plays in the primordial subject-world relation. Although he is right to suggest that exposing ourselves to such cosmic indifference is the precondition for liberation from authoritative givens, this negative interpretation of the role of the Chaos, leads to a politics of the perpetual questioning of the institutions humans create in an effort to avert their heteronomous ossification. But we also need to overcome our exclusive dependence on the indifferent if we are to re-connect with that which is unconditionally concerned with us, namely the significance of togetherness. To receive the significance of communality is not simply to move beyond (neo)liberal atomic subjectivity and more generally the abstract mode of proprietary being to which subjectivity is tied as a results of global capitalism. Rather it is to experience the expanding self characteristic of the member of the genuine collective. How does this experience inform the singular subject's relationship to the Chaos of the world? We suggest that exposure to the Chaos activates significance—communal significance and not just the subject's power of radical imaginary signification—if and when singular subjects are also exposed to the unconditional togetherness of the (un)willing collective. In this case singular subjects' willing agency is no less permeated by the call of community, rather than being thoroughly absorbed in enacting their radical imaginary powers of creating/destroying significations. Here the subject is at once willing/unwilling. In receiving the call of community, the subject's relationship to the Void, the Chaos of the world, is therefore conceivable in an entirely different way from that presumed by Castoriadis. This alternative understanding of the subject's relationship to the Chaos also has implications for the champion of radical autonomy in his dual capacity as thinker and actor in the world.

In receiving the call to community the thinker/activist receives the unconditional universal, not only of communal togetherness but also of the indifferent Void. This double receiving involves an (un)willing yet mutual informing way of thinking of each universal, communal togetherness and indifferent Void. The result is a primordial affirmation of the communal in its cosmic aloneness. This affirmation is in turn the source of the very capacity of the 'I' to say 'we', which is the presupposition of the symbolic order, that, is, it enables the very practice of creating significations or concepts. In the next two chapters we will examine Castoriadis's claims in relation to the practice of thinking autonomously with a view to exposing the hidden intellectual work of this idea of receiving significance and the implications of its denial for Castoriadis's intellectual practice. We turn next to see how this blindspot—Castoriadis's failure to appreciate the place of the idea of receiving significance—informs his reading of the inherited tradition and, in particular, skews his understanding of the limits of Plato's way of practicing philosophy.

5. NOTHING SHOCKS IN THE LABYRINTH: THE OTHER SIDE OF PLATO'S CAVE

> 'To think is not to get out of the cave; [...] To think is to enter the labyrinth'.[151]

The image of the labyrinth provides a context for appreciating Castoriadis's understanding of genuinely revolutionary thinking as unavoidably implicated in the pursuit of the political project of autonomy. For the reader who is familiar with the Platonic metaphor, Castoriadis's allusion likely calls forth the image of the ascending/descending philosopher, the unique one whose journey in and out of the cave centres on the relationship between knowledge, reality and divine truth. Yet the situation of the imprisoned cave dwellers who never exit the cave is of no less importance for Castoriadis. Presented as chained to a fixed position facing a wall that only dimly reflects shadows in the light of the cave fire, the cave dwellers symbolize the epistemic flaw of partial perspectives given that their powers of perception, imagination and understanding are severely albeit artificially curtailed. In contrasting the two images Castoriadis points to the fundamental differences between heteronomous societies as defined by the closure of meaning and (partially) open autonomous societies as the work of radical imaginary

---

151. Cornelius Castoriadis, *Crossroads in the Labyrinth*, Sussex, Harvester Press, 1984, pp. ix-x.

instituting practices. In the first section of this chapter we will return to Castoriadis's elucidation of the social-historical, including his understanding of the position of self-reflective subjects, in order to fill out the picture of the human gathering he associates with his alternative image of the labyrinth. In the second section we will revisit Castoriadis's critique of inherited thought in order to explain his reasons for thinking that Plato establishes an intellectual tradition that progressively entrenches the cave dweller's problematic approach to thinking, despite recognizing the historical nature of social being, of instituted society and of human subjects. At the heart of this approach is the desire to escape the cave. This is the same tendency Castoriadis attributes to the religious orientation. As we observed in Chapters 3 and 4, Castoriadis defines autonomous thinking as exclusively focused on the activity of creating, destroying, and the questioning that underpins these and questioning at its deepest, philosophical questioning, always emerges in relation to a particular time and place, it is unavoidably social-historical. We will suggest that for this reason the image of the labyrinth must be understood as historical in a dual sense: on one level it represents an image of social being as historical and on another it represents the outcome of the creative, destructive, questioning power of the thinker engaged in what Castoriadis calls autonomous political thinking.

In light of our reading of Castoriadis's representation of the fundamental differences between the thinking of the cave dweller and the labyrinth digger, we will go on to consider whether, despite his insistence on autonomous thinking, Castoriadis might be accused of speaking *about* autonomy, rather than meeting the demand *to think* autonomously. Through an alternative reading of the message of Plato's story of the cave, we will argue that from the standpoint of a modern-day Plato sympathizer one might reasonably reject Castoriadis's critique because, while Plato identifies the source of signification as extra-social, the story of the cave also implies that through their relationship to the philosopher the imprisoned cave dwellers may become receivers of the knowledge deriving from this source. We will suggest that this amounts to a receiving of significance over and above the social significations that Castoriadis discusses. Further, we will argue that this receiving is not of itself heteronomous in so far as it manifests what we referred to in the previous chapter as humanity's recognition of its aloneness in an indifferent world, an indifference that as we have argued Castoriadis's discussion of the political presupposes. Suggesting that the real problem with the Platonic vision is not its deference to the extra-social but its conflation of the significant and the indifferent in the idea of the supreme Good, we will develop the claim that part of the reason why Castoriadis opens himself to the objection that he fails to assign any place in his theory to social being as significant is that he rejects the notion of autonomous being as-receiving. This is why his image of the thinker as the labyrinth digger shares noteworthy similarities with the problematic democratic character of *The Republic*. With its exclusive focus on creating, destroying and questioning, Castoriadis's approach to theorizing appears rather one-sided. Indeed, we will conclude that with respect to their accounts of politically informed philosophical thinking Castoriadis and Plato emerge as two extremes, the first favouring the power of questioning to the exclusion of receiving, the second privileging the power of receiving over creation and creativity.

LABYRINTH AND CAVE AS IMAGES OF SOCIAL DOING

In juxtaposing the image of the labyrinth to that of the cave, Castoriadis affirms the mode of struggle characterizing activity taking place inside the labyrinth. The image of the labyrinth is familiar enough in the Greek tradition but Castoriadis introduces a twist in so far as he imagines the thinker who enters the labyrinth as not needing a ball of string to guide them back out. The significance of entering in no way depends upon any desire or likelihood of exiting; the point is 'to enter the labyrinth' and not to exit it. This reflects Castoriadis's approach to social doing, in general, and thoughtful doing, in particular. The figure of the labyrinth digger highlights the creative power of reflective subjects and of society. As we have already observed, this is an ontological condition: to be is to make where 'to make' means 'to create' in the radical sense of ontological creation *ex nihilo*—positing new *eidos*, new essence, new norms and laws. Nonetheless it is the contrast of this idea of thoughtful doing to the horizon of possibilities represented by the activity in and beyond the cave that brings home the point of the labyrinth metaphor. Thought that remains oriented around exiting the cave of ignorance perpetuates heteronomous thinking/being.

As we have also already observed, notwithstanding possibilities for autonomous political thinking, for the most part history consists of heteronomous modes of social being. In being defined by their heteronomous orientation to instituted society, human gatherings effectively deny the reality of historical fluidity, complexity, and unpredictability, seeking instead to validate society's social imaginary significations and the institutions embodying them, not as society's own making, but through appeal to extra-social significations, whether in the Platonic form of the eternal Good, or of Christian ideas of transcendence, or of the Marxist laws of history. In each of these cases, the effect is a closure of meaning, a halting of the democratic practice of political questioning, which results in the suppression of genuinely autonomous social-political instituting in the proper sense of the making of historical time. For Castoriadis heteronomous societies experience history - the specific reality of the human world of unceasing creation of new forms - as a restricted horizon of possibilities and as an unstable condition that must be contained, ultimately through awareness of the transcendent, the extra-social or other-worldly, covering up the field of otherness as self-making. This horizon of possibilities is represented by life within the cave of ignorance and awareness of what lies beyond.

So, in Castoriadis's thinking the ideas of autonomy and heteronomy speak not to this or that specific aspect of subjectivity or of a society's organization but to the fundamental orientations that the labyrinth and the cave represent. While society and subjectivity are always auto-poetic, indeed borrowing a phrase from Hegel, we might characterize them as the 'self-same' on this level, nonetheless, particular societies are distinguishable according to their ability to show awareness or ignorance of self-making, their defining dimension. Here, 'awareness' and 'ignorance' do not refer to a representational mode of knowing whose propositional form may or may not correctly identify its referent. Knowing is woven into the very being of society through which society gathers itself together either as reflectively relying upon its own activity of self-creation or alternatively as misrecognizing its being and the source of its doing. In constantly giving rise to these two possibilities, society manifests the conflict between the project of autonomy and the reproduction of heteronomy, between, on the one hand, accepting and rendering explicit its own self as the source of its social imaginary significations and, on the other hand, attempting to justify them and the institutions that embody them through some extra-social signification. The labyrinth and the cave illustrate these two possibilities.

It follows that Castoriadis's juxtaposition of the images of the labyrinth and the cave presupposes that they cover the same ground. Both are philosophical devices referring us to the organization of society as a whole and its relationship to the world. In Plato's story of the cave and Castoriadis's metaphor of the labyrinth, therefore, we have two competing images, not just of the philosopher, but also of the human gathering as a political project. We turn next to consider in more detail the sense in which the two images are first and foremost profoundly political and philosophical only in so far as they present competing figures of critical reflection.

THE LABYRINTH AND THE CAVE
AS SITES OF POLITICAL THINKING

> It is as political, and not philosophical, ideas that auton-
> omy, [...] the creativity of the masses, what today I would
> have called the irruption of the instituting imaginary in
> and through the activity of the anonymous collective,
> made their appearance in my writings.[152]

Castoriadis's emergence as a thinker who is positioned to
pose the fundamental question of philosophy—'what ought
we to think?'—stems from his commitment to the ideas
defining the political project of autonomy, and indeed his
reading of the importance of this project for humanity underpins his understanding of the purpose and nature of
philosophical thinking.[153] This is why in his account, the
very same contrast between heteronomy and autonomy as
modes of society also marks the modes of thinking available
to the philosopher of the western intellectual tradition. For
Castoriadis 'philosophy is a reflective activity that deploys itself both freely *and* under the constraint of its own past [...]
it is deeply historical'.[154] Castoriadis never tires of emphasiz-
ing that philosophy is at once 'uninhibited critical thought'
and a social-historical project, always belonging to a particular historical moment, and therefore unable to capture the
whole once and for all.[155]

Yet, despite the inherited intellectual tradition's potential for autonomy—despite the historical fact that the con-
stitutive elements of the project of autonomy belong to the
tradition of western modernity—it is mostly heteronomous;
in rendering itself as incapable of apprehending the essential indeterminacy of the world it remains unable to deploy
itself freely.[156] Starting with Plato, even when philosophers

---

152. Cornelius Castoriadis, *World in Fragments*, p. 371-372, our emphasis.

153. Castoriadis, *Philosophy Politics Autonomy*, p. 25.

154. Castoriadis, *Philosophy Politics Autonomy*, pp. 17-18, emphasis added.

155. Cornelius Castoriadis, *World in Fragments*, p. 337.

156. Cornelius Castoriadis, *World in Fragments*, p. 31.

acknowledge the significance of history, whether in terms of its circular movement as for Plato, or as a linear progression as for Hegel and Marx, they still 'situate themselves within history only in order to get out of it, they try to have a look at themselves from outside, they believe that they can inspect their own backs'.[157]What they fail to realize is that the thinker must remain *both* 'a flying eagle' and 'a creeping snake'. That is, even when aspiring to gain the perspective of 'the flying eagle,' the philosopher must always also stay true to the perspective of 'the creeping snake', which, as Karagiannis and Wagner observe, Castoriadis considers necessary for balancing critical distance with one's unavoidable implication in the matters being reflected upon.[158] For Castoriadis then this was one of Plato's failings, for he

> advanced the idea that there can and should be an epistēmē of politics [la politique], a sure and certain knowledge enabling one to be guided in the political domain; that, in the end, this epistēmē of statesmanship [la politique] relies upon a transcendent knowledge; and even that it relies upon transcendence itself.[159]

The philosopher of inherited thought turns out to be the one within the particular group to achieve enlightenment by stepping outside the cave, receiving the transcendent knowledge and thereby shaping his being accordingly to become its bearer in the field of politics. The philosopher of the inherited tradition seeks enlightenment through such

---

157. Castoriadis, *Crossroads in the Labyrinth*, p. xxi. For a brief overview of Castoriadis's more extensive reasons for rejecting Marx, see Chamsy Ojeili, 'Post-Marxism with Substance', pp. 233-244.

158. Nathalie Karagiannis and Peter Wagner, 'What Is to Be Thought? What Is to Be Done? The Polyscopic Thought of Kostas Axelos and Cornelius Castoriadis,' *European Journal of Social Theory*, vol. 15, no. 3, 2012, pp. 403-417 at 415 note 1.

159. Cornelius Castoriadis, *On Plato's Statesman*, Stanford, CA, Stanford University Press, 2002, p. 1. For a discussion of the implications of Catoriadis' analysis of Plato's Statesman in terms of Plato's absolutization of politics see J. Rundell, 'Autonomy, Oligarchy, Statesman: Weber, Castoriadis and the Fragility of Politics', in Vrasidas Karalis (ed.), *Cornelius Castoriadis and Radical Democracy*, Leiden and Boston: Brill, 2014, pp. 235-261 at 254-261.

a process of transcending the spaces of the cave; escaping its disturbing ground level internal organization; freeing himself from the radical incompleteness of the time of the cave and indeed nullifying time itself as the sole function of life in the cave. The expectation is that the philosopher will achieve salvation by accessing a tranquillity that only a direct appreciation of the eternal - located outside the cave - can provide and by relying upon it to reshape the political reality. Here, to think is not only to exit the cave but to return in order 'to replace the uncertainty of shadows by the clear-cut outlines of things themselves, the flame's flickering glow by the light of the true Sun'.[160] This is not to say that for Castoriadis Plato is altogether incapable of responding to the potential open-endedness of philosophical thinking through the practice of questioning.[161] Nonetheless Plato initiates an approach to thinking which grounds itself upon 'the concealment of doing and of bringing into being' in the sense discussed in previous chapters.[162]

For the purposes of the present argument it is important to note that the cave dwellers' orientation towards transcendence implicitly highlights the activity of receiving significance; we might say that their being is *to-be-as-receiving*. This is most clearly demonstrated with Plato's focus on the ascending philosopher who, having stepped outside the cave, simply basks in the light of the perfect Good and the eternal form of justice. But we can make the same observation about the prisoners who, despite never leaving the cave might themselves receive the knowledge of the eternal form of justice were they to welcome back the descending philosopher. In other words, in welcoming the Platonic philosopher as the one who has received the eternal Good and as the bearer of the knowledge of the form of justice, they too would be enacting a practice of receiving significance.[163]

160. Cornelius Castoriadis, *Crossroads in the Labyrinth*, pp. ix-x.

161. John Rundell makes this point in connection with Castoriadis's reading of Plato's *Statesman*. See John Rundell, 'Autonomy, Oligarchy, Statesman', p. 252.

162. Cornelius Castoriadis, *The Imaginary Institution of Society*, p. 373.

163. We develop this analysis in 'The Pulse of *Chronos*: Historical Time,

One might object that those who remain in the cave are not receivers in the way we are suggesting. For in rejecting the descending philosopher they fail to receive the true in so far as they remain committed to the emptiness of the dancing shadows on the walls of the cave. But even on this scenario, the fundamental difference between ignorance and enlightenment is not that between being as-receiving and being as-creating in the Castoriadian sense. For regardless of the cave dwellers' identities—whether as philosophers, as friends of the philosopher, or more broadly as members of a Castoriadian anonymous collective— the source of the true remains independent of them, both as individuals and as participants in a collective. For irrespective of their differences they would take this source to be located beyond their human world and only indirectly accessible for most of humanity. Accordingly, the difference between those who would receive the transcendent knowledge - let us say the friends of the philosopher—and those who would reject it still amounts to that between two modes of reception: one of the supposed genuine (other-worldly) truth and the other of a misrepresented (shadowy internal) reality of the cave. To be sure, the mode of reception that each individual will enact depends upon whether or not they succeed in transcending the conditions of their imprisonment, whether they come to embody the transcendent knowledge. Nonetheless the failure to do so constitutes an individual's continued implication in the pre-given mode of receiving.

By contrast, for Castoriadis, the orientation of the cave dwellers, regardless of how they might react to the philosopher, illustrates the storyteller's massive failure to appreciate that humanity is not destined passively to accept any pre-given, ready-made solutions to the challenge posed by the human need of significance. For Castoriadis Plato's construction of the story of the cave also speaks to the failure of inherited thought to recognize that the proper role of thinking is not simply that of instituting but of instituting

the Eternal and Timelessness in Platonic Gathering', *Parrhesia*, vol. 15, 2012, pp. 54-63.

through the activity of questioning the instituted. After all, even the rejection of the ideas of creation and creativity is the work of the thinker and their heteronomous society. This is why Castoriadis sees Plato as ultimately motivated by the desire to 'fix things' once and for all.[164]

> Plato [...] completely overturns the Greek conception of justice as a question that remains constantly open within the city: Who is to give what, and who is to have what? This question constantly poses the problem of distribution among the citizens and at the same time thus opens the way to further questioning. He therefore overturns this definition and makes justice what can be called and has, moreover, been called in modern times a holist, or holistic, property, a property of the whole. For Plato [...] justice is the fact that the city is well divided, well-articulated, and that, within this whole of the city, each has his place and doesn't try to obtain another one.[165]

Accordingly, for Castoriadis Plato's is the philosophical - and, in the light of subsequent historical developments, perhaps even prophetic - formulation of 'the misrecognition by society of its own being as creation and creativity' par excellence. If social being - both human subjectivity and society - is essentially autonomous and 'autonomy signifies literally and profoundly: positing one's own law for oneself,' then Plato's representation of the organization of life within the cave refuses society's capacity for autonomous self-creation, even after the return of the descending philosopher and irrespective of any subsequent reorganization. That is, the organization of the cave as defined by the instability of the shadows, the flickering of the light of the fire and the yearning for a transcendence that might enable the cave dwellers to access the benefits of the reflected light of the Sun, albeit indirectly, nonetheless smothers any possibility for rendering explicit the self-instituting power of the instituted gathering. This is because the primordial desire to achieve transcendence ultimately puts a 'freeze' on society in the sense that it stops movement by seeking to enact the eternal on

---

164. Cornelius Castoriadis, *On Plato's Statesman*, p. 5.
165. Cornelius Castoriadis, *On Plato's Statesman*, p. 2.

the collective body. In Plato's formulation of the ideal *polis*, this takes the form of a class differentiated society that assigns individuals to their pre-given positions as members of the property-owning business class, as auxiliaries and as philosopher-rulers.[166]

From the Castoriadian perspective later philosophers have arguably surpassed Plato in that they have sought to eliminate all uncertainty as to the outcome of the encounter between society conceived as the human gathering qua bearer of ignorance and the philosopher qua bearer of the truth. For in considering the likelihood that the descending philosopher might be put to death at the hands of his fellow cave dwellers, Plato had at least countenanced the thought that the cave prisoners might reject the bearer of transcendent knowledge and of the perfect Good. In contrast, by insisting on the historical reception of the word of the philosopher, no matter what - for example, by positing the inevitability of a certain revolutionary agency and/or the end of history - philosophers such as Marx and Hegel have effectively entrenched the problematic cave dweller orientation.

It is to this foundationalist reading of the intellectual tradition that Castoriadis responds with the call for an autonomous deployment of philosophy, enabling the thinker to embody society's potential for self-instituting and for questioning the instituted. For Castoriadis, to take full responsibility philosophically, as well as politically, for the unceasing creation and questioning that the proper exercise of autonomy requires is to locate oneself, individually and collectively, at the centre of an ever-expanding labyrinth:

> To think is to enter the labyrinth [...] It is to lose oneself amidst galleries which exist only because we never tire of digging them; to turn round and round at the end of a cul-de-sac whose entrance has been shut off behind us - until, inexplicably, this spinning round opens up in the surrounding walls cracks which offer passage.[167]

The philosopher of a society that rejects the aspiration to

166. Plato, *The Republic*, Penguin, 1987, Books II - IV.
167. Cornelius Castoriadis, *Crossroads in the Labyrinth*, p. x.

transcend simply acknowledges society's open dynamism, which is, at once, both here, so to speak, and beyond, never able to completely exhaust itself, given that it embodies what it alone creates and not something externally derived, whether as eternal or as universal law. Indeed, if they were fully to accept and engage with the internal instability of the cave, the cave dwellers' re-orientation would amount to effectively transforming the cave into the labyrinth. The desire for transcendence would moreover be substituted with the vision of an ever-expanding altering labyrinth. If there were an ultimate expression of humanity's salvation, this would have to be, not the act of transcendence, of exiting the cave, but that of repeating an immanent retrieval of the anonymous collective's instituting power, the perpetual creator of new *eidos* and, therefore, the ultimate questioner of its own creation. For 'the community 'receives itself' as it were, from its own past, with all that this past entails'.[168] This act of retrieval, the transformation of society by thinkingly enacting the historical, constitutes the very making of historical time. Castoriadis therefore seeks to enlighten us by dispensing with the fantasy of receiving as dreamt about by the cave dwellers and as dreamt up by their creator, Plato, and re-fantasized by the later intellectual tradition.

At the same time, Castoriadis calls upon the intellectuals of today's partially open societies to become fellow labyrinth diggers, unceasing questioners of the instituted. To respond to his call is at once to destroy the fantasy of the cave and to enter the labyrinth that the cave already is from the outset. This is why when entering the labyrinth from our current location, we cannot but find ourselves at one of its centres:

> The entrance to the labyrinth is at once one of its centers
> [...] To think is to enter the labyrinth; more exactly, it is
> to make be and appear a labyrinth when we might have
> stayed 'lying among the flowers, facing the sky'.[169]

168. Cornelius Castoriadis, 'The Greek Polis and the Creation of Democracy', p. 47.

169. Cornelius Castoriadis, Crossroads in the Labyrinth, pp. ix-x.

We have been suggesting that in preferring the questioning of significations over the creation of significance through transcendence, Castoriadis ultimately seeks to elucidate the process of the re-capturing of society's instituting power that must take place if the human/social gathering is not to be thought as fixed and instituted once and for all. By questioning we reveal to ourselves both that which is created as-created and ourselves as-creators. The practice of incessant questioning captures and re-activates the process of creating autonomously, of enacting revolutionary thinking. Here too Castoriadis gives priority to the power and activity of questioning over both that of creating/instituting and that which is created/the instituted. To the extent that we recognize ourselves as diggers of the labyrinth galleries, 'we never tire of digging' them. This tireless commitment is perhaps the only quality that distinguishes the revolutionary thinker.

For some, Castoriadis' privileging of interminable questioning indicates the merits of this approach to reasoning. For example, Alexandros Kioupkiolis argues for the superiority of Castoriadis's approach over fellow advocates of anti-foundationalist agonistic reasoning, such as Foucault, on the basis of its redeeming commitment to 'hyper-critique' understood as an approach to reasoning 'which is willing to call its founding premises into question'.[170] Defending Castoriadis against the charge of arbitrariness, Kioupkiolis insists,

> Freedom as unfettered questioning, revision and potential detachment is built into radical critical thinking. Agonistic reason could not surrender the freedom to doubt, contest, reconsider and reconfigure without

---

170. Alexandros Kioupkiolis, 'The Agonistic Turn', p. 397. Note here that 'founding premises' are not to be understood as *philosophically* founded premises, like self-evident or first principles. For Castoriadis such principles cannot be derived even from the socio-historical condition that belongs to the tradition of western modernity in constituting autonomy as a political project: 'the project of autonomy, reflection, deliberation, and reason have already been created, they are already there, they belong to our tradition. But this *condition* is not a *foundation*.' Cornelius Castoriadis, *The Castoriadis Reader*, p. 394.

> forsaking its own agonism and rationality. Standing up
> for freedom is standing up for itself.'[171]

While autonomy may be affirmed through the practice of questioning, the autonomous performance of questioning is not thereby ensured. Kioupkiolis appreciates Castoriadis's grounding of autonomy in ontology and creation of the new understood in terms of his concepts of the radical imagination and social imaginary significations.[172] However, he does not discuss how Castoriadis's analysis of the possibility of enacting autonomous thinking, the work of breaking the closure of meaning in partially open societies, involves confronting the Chaos of the world. And, as we saw in the previous chapter, awareness of the Chaos alone cannot differentiate autonomous and heteronomous practices as Castoriadis would have us believe. So, while the practice of questioning may also affirm the mode of agonistic reasoning that performs such questioning, the autonomous performance of this reasoning remains in doubt. In other words, although 'standing up for freedom' may be standing up for agonistic reason, it does not follow that the reverse is also the case. In order to examine more fully the distinctiveness of Castoriadis's intellectual practice by comparison with the inherited tradition he critiques, we turn next to reconsider Plato's exemplary story of the cave, but this time from the standpoint of a Plato sympathizer who acknowledges Castoriadis's concern that the western intellectual tradition has failed genuinely to accommodate the indeterminacy of being.

SOCIAL BEING AS RECEIVING SIGNIFICANCE

How might one respond to Castoriadis's critique from the standpoint of a Plato sympathizer? Consider the following reading of the ultimate message of Plato's story of the cave. If the cave dwellers are indeed unable to inspect their backs, to borrow Castoriadis's phrase, surely this is because they are

171. Alexandros Kioupkiolis, 'The Agonistic Turn', p.399.
172. Alexandros Kioupkiolis, 'The Agonistic Turn', p.388-389.

shackled and so others, perhaps those who control the fire, might well be in the relatively privileged position of making such an inspection. On this scenario, identifying the process by which the unshackled individual achieves self-knowing seems a reasonable task. After all, from the moment he is released until he encounters the Good outside the cave the released prisoner's journey is presented as this state of self-knowing, implicitly at first and then explicitly. Further, an important part of this painful process might be what we might describe as the initial shock that the released prisoner inevitably experiences in discovering the power to inspect and potentially to reconstitute the whole of the surrounding space of the cave through the newly gained movement of his (political) body around its own imaginary axis, a circling round that was unavailable to him as a prisoner. Castoriadis seems to underplay the transformative power of the philosopher's shock upon being freed from his fixed position.

If this potential for reconstitution is the ultimate message of the story of the cave, we can read it as suggesting that this is indeed achievable subject to acceptance of the role that the descending philosopher must play.[173] This is what is required to achieve the political liberation of the imprisoned body as a whole, to enable all to move around freely in order for them to re-create the cave's all-inclusive horizon and, in this respect, to achieve a sort of transcending of the ignorance embodied in the cave without actually exiting it. The 'new body' that would be thus created, the collective body that would now be in a position to inspect its back, so to speak, would result from a kind of leap out of the specificity of the cave of ignorance. Here the political challenge that Castoriadis insists upon, to create new *eidos* in response to alterity, is achieved with the emergence of a new bodily movement out of the fullness of the prisoners' fixed position, but it is also grounded on a transformative shock linked not just to transformation, but to a transcending activity whose power Castoriadis denies.

---

173. We develop this interpretation of the significance of the story of the cave in 'The Pulse of *Chronos*'.

Next let us focus on the destruction/creation relation in order to explore a decisive difference between Castoriadis and Plato, namely that between creating the new and receiving the eternal. One particular moment in *The Republic* implicitly points to the possibility of an apocalyptic destruction of the structure underlying all forms of imperfectly instituted society. This moment arises with the countenancing of the possibility that the prisoners in the cave might recognize the descending philosopher as their gatherer and welcome him as such. This sort of welcoming would permit them at once: to destroy the institutions of ignorance; to gather indeterminately around the philosopher; and, ultimately, to re-institute their society by receiving and embodying the form of the just *polis* that the philosopher brings from the outside world, that which is informed by the eternal forms and the supreme Good. In the story of the cave the fundamental structure of ignorance, that which also characterizes all modes of imperfect society - from Timarchy through Oligarchy and Democracy to Tyranny[174]- presupposes the differentiation between the gathering of the prisoners who misrecognize knowledge of the shadows as knowledge of what is genuinely true and those who control the deceptive institutions, the distribution of the light of the fire through which the shadows appear. This differentiation positions individuals in relation to the reality of the cave as a whole.

The interesting point to note here is that for Plato life in the cave is possible precisely because humanity is the exclusive bearer of self-concern. By comparison with something like the Christian gathering that defers to the care of a loving God, the Platonic gathering does not point to a self-concerned extra-social source; there is no other-worldly self-concerned being in the cosmic order. Accordingly, humanity is conceived as absolutely alone and thus immanently capable of either fully appreciating or misunderstanding the radical nature of this aloneness. In this case, society is in an implicit or explicit struggle to enact the mode of being either of ignorance or of enlightenment. As we noted above, in

---

174. Plato, *The Republic*, paragraphs 545d-576c.

the story of the cave the primordial expression of ignorance manifests as the indeterminate gathering of the prisoners whose false knowledge stems from their being chained in a restrictive position. As such this gathering, although exclusively self-concerned, is nevertheless not in a position to affirm its aloneness in the cosmos. Given their state of ignorance, the cave dwellers' primary challenge is not so much to create their institutions anew but to receive their being as this pre-reflective self-concern of the collective. For only this receiving will enable them to become both destroyers of the institutions of ignorance and creators of society's new institutions. For Plato the indeterminate gathering of the cave dwellers must become transcending if it is to dwell in the depth of its aloneness. For if a human society is truly alone in the cosmos and hence significant only due to its own self-affirming, then that which is beyond can only be the absolutely and hence perfectly indifferent. Plato emphasizes that the beyond, the indifferent, is also supremely significant; it is the Good, which is beyond being and beyond knowing, or in Castoriadis's terms, beyond signification. Ultimately in affirming itself by receiving the perfect Good, society elevates its aloneness and transforms it into a receiving of significance thereby positing itself as being beyond signification. To be as gathered in this pure sense is thus the beginning and the end of the members of the indeterminate gathering.

From the above it follows that being-as-concerned is primordially manifested as society's power to point to: the absolutely indifferent as the source of an overflowing perfection that offers its timeless significance; the eternal being of the forms; the conceptual knowing of the philosopher; and ultimately the being in time of society that becomes the gathering qua receiving of the Good. Society thus constitutes the very power to withstand its imperfect or finite being-as-concerned by transforming itself into the field of the pure collective receiving of the significance of that which is indifferent and hence of its own pure enactment of togetherness as significant. In this way, to be-as-concerned is the most radical expression of finitude that, by taking itself to its limit, reveals the infinite in its own being.

From this perspective, transcendence is indeed the ultimate aim of the human gathering, but this means to seek and to identify the ultimate source of the activation of concern in the indifference of the cosmos that is at once supremely significant and the source of significance. This is why humanity becomes a self-concerned project whose aim it is to gather itself in its pure indeterminacy. Moreover, society is taken to gather in its aloneness in an original and originating way only by receiving the cosmic, the unconditionally perfect indifference, in whose horizon the human gathering must be situated in the absence of any predetermining givens. Society's receiving serves as the process through which it can overcome its instituted ignorance, whereas its primordial gathering positions it to institute itself in a way that is fully informed by its aloneness in the cosmos. In this state, then, the gathering becomes a destructive force in overcoming its history through the pure receiving of the Good.

In the story of the cave the philosopher's ascent to the outside world manifests the gathering's power to immanently transcend the given order of the cave. The philosopher's subsequent descent back into the cave to rejoin his fellow cave dwellers gives rise to the primordial indeterminate gathering and its power either to affirm or to reject its mode of being as receiving. But in escaping, the philosopher is the unique one who at once belongs to the gathering and points to the possibility of the gathering's liberation from the state of ignorance. On his return he is both like and unlike everyone else given that he re-enters the cave not only as the bearer of the knowledge of the eternal form of the just gathering, a knowledge that he can share with others, but also as the bearer of the idea of the perfect indifferent and supremely significant Good. To welcome the philosopher as we noted above is thus to destroy the order of the cave and to re-form the human gathering as a project within the field of the gathering's aloneness and as informed by the philosopher's unique journey. Accordingly, the idea of the enlightened philosopher's return to the cave anticipates an intellectual practice grounded in the separation of the intellectual from the masses, like the Leninist notion of a revolutionary vanguard of the people, which Castoriadis opposes assigning the intellectual to 'a humanity in which s/he is only one atom' while 'history is the domain in which there unfolds the creativity of *all* people'.[175]

For reasons that we need not examine here, Plato links the philosopher's status as the unique one to the gathering as exclusively particular in that the gathering is limited to the gathering of the *polis* and this association precludes the Platonic gathering from serving as the source of its own indeterminacy.[176]Indeterminacy as such is thus implicitly posited as being located beyond; this is why it must somehow be brought to the gathering. At the same time, the members of the gathering are not equally positioned to engage in the necessary transcendence because this presupposes that the gathering as a whole is positioned to transcend the limitations of its particularity by entering he universal place of the a-conceptual good. The tension created by the demand for transcendence within the unavoidably particular gathering is resolved when one member—the unique one—moves beyond the particularity of the gathering and then returns to affirm this particularity. Neither the significance nor the indifference of the Good can be equally accessed by all the members of the gathering, for this would require each one of them to transcend the particularity of their gathering. At the fundamental level of the pure affirmation of the indeterminacy of the gathering, only the Platonic philosopher brings to the collective the idea or form of the gathering, given that he alone is the bearer of the gathering's reflective element. At the same time, since the philosopher's aim is to affirm the particularity of the gathering, he arrives as the bearer of the idea of the gathering that is limited by particularity.

175. Cornelius Castoriadis, *Philosophy Politics Autonomy*, p. 12, emphasis added.

176. We develop these ideas in *The Rebellious Gathering: Plato's Republic and the End of Philosophy*, book manuscript in progress.

From the above it follows that in order to emerge as the pure indeterminate gathering that institutes itself, this gathering must depend upon that which is beyond both to affirm its indeterminacy and to access the idea of gathering. The receiving that Plato elaborates is thus problematic in so far as it insists on the gathering's being as particular. This however still leaves open the question of whether the status of the gathering as receiving and, more specifically, as receiving significance, precludes it from participating in the sort of creative/destructive instituting of society that Castoriadis advocates when the primordial gathering is conceived as universal.

SOCIAL BEING AS PRIVILEGING CREATIVITY OVER THE RECEPTION OF SIGNIFICANCE

Castoriadis's conceptual framework implies that the creation/destruction involved in society's autonomous self-institution is contradicted by any suggestion that the indeterminate gathering of the anonymous collective must not only gather itself in its own indeterminacy - as Castoriadis would agree - but it must also position itself as-receiving significance. This is because Castoriadis conflates the possibility of receiving significance in and as members of the gathering with an admittedly problematic mode of receiving signification. From this perspective he represents the cave as fundamentally suited to the gathering of subjects defined by the desire to escape and the labyrinth as suited to those defined by the awareness of the very absence of any such desire. But, as we saw in the previous section, the cave is the dwelling place of subjects who aspire to transform the being of the gathering into *an exclusive receiving*—recall that the members of the gathering are denied equal power to access the significant. We want to suggest next that Castoriadis's labyrinth digger conversely aspires to become *an exclusive creating*/instituting, that is, a creating/instituting without receiving. Let us try to develop this point by comparing the bodily movement of the labyrinth digger to that of the liberated prisoner, the philosopher who, as we argued above, undergoes a radical transformation following the shock of coming to embrace the totality of the cave by circling around.

The first thing to note about a labyrinth digger is that curiously, nothing can surprise them since their ability to move around, to dig and keep digging, is grounded in an incessant power of questioning that fuels the digger's movement. Unlike the Platonic cave dweller's experience of circling the cave, the labyrinth digger's movement seems incapable of triggering a radically altering experience in that nothing seems capable of shocking them—similarly to the way that the newly released cave dweller might be shocked as a result of their circling movement. Following Castoriadis's account of the autonomous thinker, the digger is, of course, supposed to be radically self-altering. As Gourgouris explains, self-alteration understood as internalized otherness in the sense of a psychical force of alteration, is key to Castoriadis's understanding of the process of subject formation and hence of the subject's capacity for political autonomy.[177] Nonetheless, despite the perpetual change of 'landscape' inside the labyrinth, one thing seems to remain constant and unaffected by any sort of alteration. This is the digger qua political being or, in other words, Castoriadis's questioner. But if nothing is greater, so to speak, than the power to be as a digger/questioner then it would appear that nothing can make the digger expand in a manner that might position them to embrace the surrounding horizon. Our second observation then is that the labyrinth digger's bodily movement lacks the power, not only to be shocked by what it encounters, but also to expand in relation to that encountered. Castoriadis insists that the labyrinth digger is always located at the centre of the labyrinth, which is in turn wherever they happen to be digging. But the contrast with the cave dweller suggests that the labyrinth digger is their own centre. Concentrating on their apparently impenetrable singularity, they appear to remain forever unchallenged and indeed unchallengeable at this level. So, their position as a digger is fixed to this extent even though everything around them changes. Contrary to Castoriadis's intentions, here we can detect an ontological closure in the constitution of subjectivity in direct correspondence with the closure of meaning that arises with the privileging of questioning that we outlined earlier, a closure that dictates that everything created is to be destroyed.

Given these observations, we might ask whether the labyrinth digger has more in common, than Castoriadis is prepared to acknowledge, with the initial image of the imprisoned Platonic cave dweller - the prisoner prior to the moment of liberation. Might it not be the case that the labyrinth digger also engages in misrecognizing the perpetual movement of the shadows and the flickering of the light, seeing these instead as the ever-changing labyrinth, despite a greater flexibility of movement? If so then the mode of reflective subjectivity that the image of the labyrinth digger reveals remains problematic, despite Castoriadis's aspirations. This would explain the regrettable similarities between the identity of Castoriadis's labyrinth digger and Plato's 'democratic character', the problematic type of individual that flourishes in a democratic regime.[178] In *The Republic* Plato introduces the democratic character as a point of contrast with the just individual in the context of the discussion of democracy, the latter being a form of 'imperfect society' that emerges with the inevitable failure of the genuinely just city to sustain itself. The democratic form thus arises from elements that result from the dissolution of the just *polis*. Nothing holds these new elements together except their sheer willingness to be together; they are united in a non-binding and non-hierarchical way. Perhaps we could read Plato's discussion of democracy as drawing attention to what we might call the dictatorship of new *eidos*, in the Castoriadian sense of the

---

178. Plato, *The Republic*, paragraphs 558d-562.

latter, precisely because within democracy it is conceivable that new forms are capable of being endlessly created, questioned and destroyed. As we saw in chapter 2, in a genuinely democratic regime, forms are indeed liberated from their association with extra-social significations, from their explicit reliance on a (quasi-)religious dimension. But we might also think that they present consistently with the fluidity of the shadows of the cave. Of course, for Castoriadis Plato is the 'archenemy of democracy' and so there is no reason to be guided by his analysis.[179] Still Plato's critique of democracy is informed by his assessment of the mode of being of a society whose fundamentals match the features of the Athenian *polis*, which, as we noted in Chapter 2, Castoriadis takes to be the first historical instance of an explicitly autonomous society. To this extent, we are justified in exploring any similarities between Castoriadis's labyrinth digger and what Plato describes as the democratic character, even though the democratic character that is the subject of Plato's scorn resembles the contemporary consumerist conceptions of subjectivity from which, as we also saw in Chapter 2, Castoriadis distances his own ideal. Let us turn then to the specific qualities that Plato assigns to the democratic character.

According to Plato, the democratic character, understood as someone 'who believes in liberty and equality,' is fundamentally incapable of making any principled distinction between 'necessary' and 'unnecessary' desires - 'desires we can't avoid or whose satisfaction benefits us' and those 'which cannot be got rid of with practice'.[180] Such a character will inevitably tend to treat all pleasures as equal in their demand for satisfaction. Ultimately 'the democratic man' is defined by capriciousness:

> he lives from day to day, indulging the pleasure of the moment. One day it's wine, women and song, the next water to drink and a strict diet; one day it's hard physical training, the next indolence and careless ease, and then

179. Castoriadis, 'The Greek *Polis* and the Creation of Democracy', p. 46.

180. Plato, *The Republic*, paragraph 559e.

a period of philosophic study. Often he takes to politics and keeps jumping to his feet and saying or doing whatever comes into his head. Sometimes all his ambitions and efforts are military, sometimes they are all directed to success in business. There is no order or restraint in his life, and he reckons his way of living is pleasant, free and happy, and sticks to it through thick and thin.[181]

The resemblance to Castoriadis's labyrinth digger becomes readily apparent when we take into account Castoriadis's valorization of individuals' willing when attempting to explain the radical transformative power characterizing the autonomous collective as we discussed in Chapter 4. This raises the question whether Castoriadis's labyrinth digger shares a bit too much with the pseudo-democratic figure who is the subject of both Plato's and Castoriadis's scorn. After all, both can be seen as permeated with narcissistic emptiness if, as we have argued, nothing can shock their being. Just as the labyrinth digger moves from one gallery to the next, so too the democratic character moves from the pursuit of one pleasure to the next. In both cases it is only subjects' own willing that links them to specific choices/desires. In participating in the process of creating significations of various sorts, both lack any binding link to the source of signification, the significant that would enable them to move in some principled way and this despite Castoriadis's insistence on the rule of self-limitation.

Given the above, Castoriadis's anti-Platonism arguably renders him an inverted Plato. For on close inspection, we notice that like Plato, Castoriadis draws our attention to a kind of apocalyptic destruction of the given order; this is the labyrinth for Castoriadis and the cave for Plato. But where Plato insists upon receiving without allowing for the creativity of instituting, Castoriadis insists upon instituting in a way that privileges questioning over receiving the instituted. In a sense, we almost have a case of extended historical double negation. Whereas Plato negates democracy and establishes the heteronomy of the Platonic cave, in theorizing

---

181. Plato, *The Republic*, paragraph 561d.

the modern version of the project of autonomy Castoriadis negates Platonism while restoring a modern version of Athenian democracy.

CONCLUSION

Despite proposing the image of the labyrinth digger as a way of highlighting the role of reflective subjects in enacting society's potential for autonomous creative/self-institution, Castoriadis's juxtaposition of this image to that of the cave dweller ultimately renders his own thought as the other equally problematic extreme of the Platonic vision he rejects. If, as we have argued, the cave and the labyrinth represent two ways of conceiving both the political project of autonomy—of instituting society as explicitly self-instituting—and the quality of the revolutionary thinking, it becomes possible to ask 'who needs the cave and who needs the labyrinth?' In exploring the Castoriadian and Plato sympathizer's responses to this question we have seen that Castoriadis overlooks an important dimension of the cave dwellers' situation that this mode of gathering gives rise to the possibility of receiving significance. We have suggested that Plato's inability to see the gathering as the source of its own significance stems from his conflation of the source of value with the indifferent world. Castoriadis by contrast conceives the indifference of the world in terms of the Chaos that is devoid of significance. But unlike Plato he fails to make room in his theory for any conception of social being as significant and this leads him to privilege the power of questioning, creating and destroying with which the collectivity of willing singularities is identified. Without any possibility of moving beyond their willing subjectivity to a mode of receiving, the members of the gathering as creators of their own significance, Castoriadis's labyrinth diggers can be shown inadvertently to share the features of a pseudo-democratic subjectivity. Having identified the limitations of Castoriadis's mode of philosophical thinking as regards its potential to illuminate an implicit notion of receiving significance, we turn finally to examine Castoriadis's formulation of philosophy's fundamental question.

6. 'WHAT OUGHT WE TO THINK?': THE LIMITS OF CASTORIADIS'S THINKING

According to Castoriadis,

> [...] the object of philosophy is the question: What ought I, what ought we, to think—about being, about knowledge of Being, about 'I', about 'we,' about our polity, about justice etc..[182]

Our aim in this chapter is to assess the implications of Castoriadis' formulation of the question for philosophy in the light of his commitment to the project of autonomy. As we saw in the previous chapter, Castoriadis attributes to the practice of genuine theorizing a similar role to being autonomous as in the case of political action. Having been 'born in and through the *polis*' and being 'part of the same movement which brought about the first democracies', philosophy is, for Castoriadis, a 'central element of the Greco-western project of individual and social autonomy'.[183] Granting Castoriadis's insistence on the centrality of the project of autonomy for both political action and philosophical thinking, what must such thinking involve, how does it begin and how should it develop?

We will suggest that, while the intensity involved in Castoriadis's elucidation of the subject matter of philosophy is powerful enough to render explicit the field and initial task for philosophical thinking (hereafter 'thinking'),

---

182. Cornelius Castoriadis, *Philosophy Politics Autonomy*, p. 25.

183. Cornelius Castoriadis, *Philosophy Politics Autonomy*, p. 13-15. For a discussion see Suzi Adams, 'Interpreting creation', pp. 25-41.

paradoxically, in exposing the centrality of the question of *what* ought to be thought, it also reveals why this focus on the subject matter of philosophy does not exhaust the question of thought. At least implicitly and rather vaguely, Castoriadis shows some appreciation that the fundamental question of thinking points beyond its 'what' formulation. Yet, precisely because the question 'what ought we to think' is fundamental, his own formulation turns out to be rather limited and this in turn has certain negative implications for his particular response to the fundamental question. More specifically, we will argue: (1) that there is a tension in Castoriadis's acknowledgement of the retreat of the political project of autonomy, on the one hand, and its thinkability as a viable project, on the other; and (2) that this tension remains unresolved in so far as Castoriadis fails to recognize the effects of the project's retreat on the thinker who must be understood as the bearer of the place of the project's retreat.

In order to develop our argument we will begin by examining Castoriadis's claims regarding the task of the philosopher against the background of the terms that are implied by his formulation of the question for philosophy. Then, through an examination of Castoriadis's discussion of the current retreat of the political project of autonomy, we will identify the contours of a Castoriadian response to the fundamental question that acknowledges what we call its 'where' and 'when' dimensions. Here we will suggest that this acknowledgement also effectively commits the thinker to thinking the very (im)possibility of the autonomous collective as the more precisely defined subject matter for thinking.

After examining Castoriadis's response to the question 'what ought we to think?', namely the project of collective autonomy, in terms of his response to the 'where' and 'when' dimensions of the fundamental question for philosophy we will move on to argue that Castoriadis's acknowledgement of the retreat of the political project ultimately commits him to the view that the political retreat must be transformed into a *philosophical* retreat and this can be achieved when the retreat of the collective happens *in the thinker*, so to speak.

PHILOSOPHICAL THINKING

'What ought I, what ought we to think?' To be sure, when philosophical thinking emerges it seeks its proper subject matter. But the implication here is that genuine thinking always appears as if for the first time and thus encounters itself by asking the same fundamental question. Of course, the question arises anew in the context of the given social-historical moment. As we noted in Chapter 5, Castoriadis's conception of philosophy, his response to the question of 'what self-reflective activity is about', is explicitly informed by the subject matter of his own philosophy, a philosophy of the social-historical that is formulated in part through his critical reading of the history of western philosophy. From this perspective the ancient philosophers' challenge is still very much with us today. That is, the proper focus of philosophy is neither the Heideggerian question of the meaning of being, nor the Cartesian practice of doubting, a practice that is undertaken by an insecure subjectivity overwhelmed by the instability and relativity of meanings. The focus of philosophy should not even be the Kantian question of the conditions of possibility for knowledge. None of these approaches can serve to formulate the proper question for thinking in so far as this latter is in the primordial state of encountering itself and attempting to identify its mission and place in the modern epoch. Instead the question, 'what ought we to think?' invokes an inquiry into fundamentals, which both springs from and points to a state of collective being shaped through the exercise of radical autonomous thinking and in relation to the thinker's activity of thinking in connection with the current condition of humanity. Indeed, in focusing our attention on how the exercise of radical autonomy affects the very character of thinking, Castoriadis implies that the very asking of the question itself gives rise to a sceptical attitude toward the claim of any subject matter to be pre-given. In raising the question then, in seeking the proper subject matter of philosophy, the questioner is already at a distance from the subject-centred Cartesian tradition of piecemeal doubting; they encounter their thinking through the activity of having already rejected any predetermined grounding in some given subject matter. It is in this sense that for Castoriadis, philosophy is reflecting freely or 'uninhibited critical thought.'[184]

With this observation in mind and before turning to Castoriadis's response to the question as posed, let us consider the implied parameters of the question itself. Firstly, in asking 'what ought we to think', and in so far as the question invites a response, our attention is inevitably drawn to *that which matters*, the significant. That is, on the face of it we are invited to think something like: 'we ought to think what matters'. But, if we agree that thinking as thinking is the pure intentionality towards recognizing and embracing *what matters*, our response inevitably leads to further questions. From where, for instance, would thinking get its call, so to speak, to think what matters? In the absence of such a call, thinking would be at a loss; in seeking the subject matter for thinking, the thinker would be forced into a disoriented state of having *to think prior to thinking*. Whatever the idiosyncratic significance of such an effort for the thinker, in order for thinking to think *what matters* more broadly, for the collective, or universally in some suitable sense of this term, it must belong somehow to that which at the same time as informing thinking, is in a sense *beyond* the thinking in question given that it constitutes the object for thinking, the *that* which matters for thinking. So, thinking must get its call to think *from what matters* itself. But now the relation we have just identified—of what matters as being beyond thinking—indicates clearly the question of a place for thinking as well as for what matters. It follows that thinking what matters, presupposes a relating to and acknowledgement of a 'where'. We must accordingly supplement Castoriadis's 'what' question with a reference to the implied

---

184. Cornelius Castoriadis, *World in Fragments*, p. 337.

'where' question: 'What ought we to think and *where* ought we to be situated in order to think it?'

Even this expanded version of the question, however, is still not broad enough to capture the full significance of the fundamental question for philosophy in the Castoriadian frame. As already noted, Castoriadis emphasises not only the social but also the *historical* situatedness of the thinker:

> I cannot ignore the fact that my own thought, however, original I may deem it to be, is but a ripple, at best a wave, in the huge social historical stream which welled up in Ionia twenty-five centuries ago. I am under the double imperative: think freely and to think under the constraint of history.[185]

So, we must add at least one further dimension: 'What ought we to think? Where and *when* ought we to think it?' But if the 'what', the 'where' and the 'when' of the question of philosophy are not givens for the autonomous thinker that Castoriadis aspires to be, then, following this approach the thinking in question cannot allow itself to be subject to the limits of the identitary logic and ontology that govern the inherited philosophical tradition. For Castoriadis, as we have seen, inherited thought, from Plato to Descartes, Marx and Heidegger, is incapable of thinking by reference to the terms of an essentially indeterminate world. It follows that from Castoriadis's perspective the thinker's *mode of thinking*, the 'how' of the activity of thought, is no less implicated in the formulation of the fundamental question for philosophy.

From this preliminary exploration of Castoriadis's formulation of the fundamental question we have arrived at a more complicated formulation, which we can refer to as 'the what-where-when-how question'. The 'what', 'where', 'when', and 'how' of thinking constitute four indispensable dimensions of the question that activates genuine thinking. They are unavoidably implicated in the task that Castoriadis assigns the philosopher qua philosopher, namely 'the task of thinking what is to be thought'.[186] Taking this multidimen-

---

185. Cornelius Castoriadis, *Philosophy Politics Autonomy*, p. 19.
186. Cornelius Castoriadis, *The Imaginary Institution*, p. 222.

sional question as the question for autonomous thinking, in the sense of the philosophical question that opens the field of radical autonomous (self)reflection in Castoriadis's terms, enables us to say: The challenge for thinking is to think what matters in a manner that matters in a place and time that matter. Having considered Castoriadis's response to the 'how' dimension of the fundamental question in the previous chapter, here we will examine Castoriadis's response to these other dimensions. However, one more observation is in order concerning the terms in which the fundamental question for philosophy has been raised.

THINKING AND THE (UN)WILLING COLLECTIVE

We noted above that if we are to think what matters in a manner that matters then our thinking must somehow belong to what is to be thought; it must be activated by and in it as the thinking that itself matters. We might say that thinking is the intensification, the deepening or expansion of this very belonging, which is articulated by the 'what-where-when-how' of thinking. If so, then the 'what-where-when-how question' already presupposes an affirmative answer to the prior question: 'ought we to think at all?' ('the 'ought' question'). An affirmative answer to the 'ought' question is implied by the very act of asking the 'what' question. That is, to ask Castoriadis's question is to imply a response to the 'ought' question; it is to position oneself in relation to a single affirmative answer. The 'ought' question is unavoidably prior because, unlike the 'what-where-when-how' question, it invokes the singular being of the thinker and their relation to what matters. This is the fundamental pre-condition for the activation of thinking as that whose questioning is concerned with what matters in a manner that matters. In other words, the 'ought' question affirms genuine thinking as that of the impersonal in the personal and thus presupposes the singularity of the thinker as a field of commitment and associated willingness to think in a way that takes the thinker's political and philosophical commitment beyond its grounding in a strictly personal willing. That is, it situates the thinker in the happening of the radical affirmation of their significant singularity qua participant of the collective. This relationship of affirmation explains why, as Castoriadis admits political thinking cannot justifiably remain within the limits of a pure decisionism.

So thinking and its questioning presuppose the situatedness and emergence of the singularity of the thinker in what matters, or more precisely, they presuppose the singular subject's *transformation* into one who matters qua thinker precisely because this is what it would mean for one's thinking to belong to what matters. So what matters also has the power to transform the singular subject into one who matters as a thinker and who is in turn empowered, in this capacity of a significant thinker, to transform what matters into a subject matter for thinking. An implied affirmative response to the 'ought' question gives rise to what we will refer to as 'the committed thinker', the one who emerges in their capacity as already associated with what matters in the appropriate way. In focusing their thinking on developing a response to 'the what-where-when-how question', the committed thinker is already claimed by what matters and is on the way to thinking in this very capacity. The commitment, 'yes, we must think' thus frames Castoriadis's fundamental question accordingly: 'Since we ought to think (what matters), what ought we to think and where, when and how ought we to think it?'

So far, we have suggested that in recognizing Castoriadis's aspiration to be as a committed thinker, we can attribute to him an affirmative response to the 'ought' question, which is implied by a certain formulation of the 'what' question, a view about what is appropriate as the subject matter of philosophy. Being unwilling, in the sense of being claimed by what matters or being-as-receiving, provides thinking with its significance because to think is to recognize the belonging of the thinker's singularity to what matters. Being claimed as a thinker by what matters, one is posited as a *significant* thinker, one who receives the call to think and hence as already positioned to think what matters in the appropriate place and time. If, however, what matters does indeed render the thinker as significant—if what matters claims the thinker and their activity as belonging to what matters—then there is a sense in which this relation already provides thinking with its subject matter, including the place, time and mode of its happening. That is, if and when thinking is to take up the challenge to think, it would already appear to have been drawn to do so, not by awareness of the fundamental questions in the abstract but by the answers, which they elicit. This is why, in spite of any appearances to the contrary, Castoriadis's prior commitment to the political project of autonomy does not thereby commit his thinking to treating the project of autonomy as a given. When, for example, as we saw in Chapter 5, Castoriadis insists that 'autonomy, [...] the creativity of the masses, [...] the irruption of the instituting imaginary in and through the activity of the anonymous collective' entered his writing as political rather than philosophical ideas, he could be accused of taking for granted the political project of autonomy. But this would be a mistake. Although his formulation of the question for philosophy follows from and as a development of his commitment to the political project of autonomy, from the perspective we are exploring, the question that the thinker raises comes *after* the answer as a way of reminding one that the real challenge springs from the answer which must be *thinkingly articulated*. In other words, the thinker is already familiar with the answer, albeit as the project of autonomy to be thinkingly elaborated. This answer is *unwilling* in the sense that its existence does not depend on activation of individual and collective willing, but rather depends on an unconditional receiving of the call to community that is informed, as we have suggested, by the Void.

Returning to Castoriadis's response to the 'what' question, we can summarize as follows. The combined effect of what we referred to above as the 'ought' and the 'what' questions is the emergence of the thinker as one who is committed to the project of autonomy. Moreover, the radical willing associated with this project is the only genuine self-presencing that the singular subject can enact, provided that they do so as a participant in the political collective. When thinking is genuinely informed by these two aspects—the subject's prior commitment and the mutual informing of the individual and the collective—it functions as 'society's thinking as making itself' in way that produces society's transformation from heteronomy to autonomy. For Castoriadis, it is this sort of autonomous, yet mostly implicit, transformative becoming that the committed thinker is called upon to elucidate in the appropriate ontological-political terms, the terms, as we have seen, of creation/destruction of *eidos* as a response to otherness.

THE RETREAT OF THE POLITICAL PROJECT OF AUTONOMY

Let us grant that the political project of autonomy is the proper subject matter for the committed thinker; that the thought in question—autonomous thinking—also *belongs to* such a (partially open) society, or to the collective, rather than to the thinker in their uniqueness; and that the thinker's critical distance from the heteronomy of their society's mode of being is made possible in and through their activity as a self-reflecting subjectivity and creator of new ideas. This approach permits us to ask the question, in the light of the discussion so far: 'when and where is the autonomous collective manifested in the critical thought of the thinker as that which matters?' To put the same question in a different way: 'How does Castoriadis address the 'where' and 'when' dimensions of the fundamental question for thinking?' 'What is the *topos* of his response?'

Castoriadis's discussion of the situation of the fate and prospects of the political project of autonomy in the 'modern' period offers scope for identifying the contours of a response to the 'where' and 'when' aspects of the question for

thinking. Castoriadis considers the prospects for the realization of the project of autonomy in the context of a diagnosis
of the modern period, which he defines in terms of:

> the conflict, but also the mutual contamination and en-
> tanglement, of two imaginary significations: autonomy,
> on the one hand, unlimited expansion of 'rational mas-
> tery', on the other'.[187]

As regards the fate and prospects of the project of autonomy
in the last two centuries, he concludes that this period:

> has proved the radical inadequacy [...] of the programs
> in which it [the project of autonomy] had been embodied
> [...] That the demonstration of this inadequacy in actual
> historical fact is one of the roots of present political apa-
> thy and privatization hardly needs stressing. For the re-
> surgence of the project of autonomy, new political objec-
> tives and new human attitudes are required.[188]

Here Castoriadis identifies the failure of the political project of autonomy with the shortcomings of the various political programs that have embodied it over time. Nonetheless,
a resurgence of the project is not just a matter of calling
for participation in more viable political programs. In acknowledging the retreat of the political project of autonomy,
Castoriadis does not also claim to identify some viable political program for the project's re-activation. Indeed, if such
genuine options were still available within the modern heteronomous world of global capitalism, the focus would prop-
erly be on the strictly political question of how best to ex-
ploit them. Instead Castoriadis insists that the demand upon

---

187. Cornelius Castoriadis, *World in Fragments*, p. 37.

188. Cornelius Castoriadis, *World in Fragments*, p. 43. Having situated
Castoriadis's 'utopian vision of a socialist political community within the
tradition of post-Marxism', Ojeili attributes Castoriadis's understanding
of the contemporary retreat of the project of autonomy to his failure to
recognize elements of this projects in the postmodern thought of Derrida,
Laclau and Mouffe, Butler or Spivak. See Chamsy Ojeili, 'Post-Marxism
with Substance', pp. 238-239. However, Ojeili's observation shows a
misunderstanding about the social-political site of the retreat Castoriadis
discusses. Ojeili doesn't seem to take account of Castoriadis's insistence on
giving priority to political thinking tied to the creativity of the anonymous
collective over intellectual work that speaks about such political thinking.

the committed thinker is to create 'new political objectives'. Here the emphasis appears to be on the question: 'what are we to do?' But this is the question that follows from 'what are we to think?'[189] It is the question for the thinker qua activist. Nevertheless, paradoxically in the light of the retreat that he acknowledges, we can infer that given Castoriadis's recognition of the gravity and the extent of the failure of the political programs to date, even reflecting upon the creation of new political programs may be premature. The challenge arising for the thinker qua philosopher, the challenge for the thinker in thinking autonomy *philosophically,* is to follow through the implications of acknowledging the absence of any visible options for a re-activation of the political project. Ultimately, this is the social-historical context that gives rise to the challenge that the committed thinker of autonomy must face. Being committed to the political project in the current conditions, one must *thinkingly create* the (idea of the) autonomous collective, the social-historical gathering of free individuals as creators of their society, and this thinking must be enacted as integral to the realization of the project of autonomy itself.

To repeat, Castoriadis situates this philosophical task of thinking autonomy, not just within the context of the political project's retreat but at the very historical moment when such retreat has confirmed the absence of any visible political alternatives. It would seem then that the depth and the extent of the political failure forces the thinker to ask the philosophical question of *the possibility as such* of the project of autonomy. Castoriadis seems to acknowledge as much in the way he dismisses as 'fictive' the suggestion that the project of autonomy might be impossible:

> As far as our eyes can see, nothing allows us to affirm that a self-transformation of history such as this is impossible; no place—except the fictive and finally incoherent non-place of identitary logic-ontology—exists where the one who could assert this could possibly stand.[190]

189. Cornelius Castoriadis, *Philosophy Politics Autonomy*, p. 25.
190. Cornelius Castoriadis, *The Imaginary Institution*, p. 373.

What is interesting to note here is that Castoriadis distinguishes between the 'place/non-place' of autonomy and identitary logic-ontology respectively. These two modes of thought are not contrasted in the abstract. Rather, they belong to two different ways of experiencing the social-historical gathering that situates them respectively in their 'place' and 'non-place'. That is, in the current historical moment, the imaginary significations of autonomy and the unlimited expansion of rational mastery are related respectively to the collapse of the project of autonomy and the triumph of heteronomy. Nevertheless, despite the appearance that the project of rational mastery has been victorious over that of autonomy and just when history shows itself to be resistant to self-transformation, Castoriadis insists that it is the thinking of autonomy that is appropriately placed to affirm this possibility.

But if, as we have argued above, the thinking in question must be integral to the project of autonomy then it must be integral to the project's historical collapse. This raises the question: 'what is the place of a thinking that is sufficiently empowered to affirm the meaning and possibility of the project of autonomy despite history's apparent verdict?' It seems that the only available historically informed place from which to undertake the autonomous thinking of autonomy is the site of the very failure of the project itself. Where other than at the site of the project's retreat and, hence, of the associated acknowledgement of the project of autonomy as having retreated, might the thinker situate himself/herself in order to enact the philosophical project? If the thinker is to elucidate the very meaning of the possibility (or impossibility) of autonomy as such he/she must do so at the site of the complete failure of all empirical possibilities for the radical emancipation of humanity that the last two centuries have witnessed. For it is here that the committed thinker must aspire to encounter the autonomous collective as such.

The place of the retreat of the autonomous collective is a place in which it becomes possible for the gathering to take place, so to speak, as something not reducible to a mere empirical observation about failed political programs. As such it would no longer be rendered invisible through its identification with the various historically failed political programs. Moreover, it is at this point that the committed thinker might face the most radical of historical challenges to the project of autonomy, namely the possibility of having to affirm *the impossibility* of history's radical self-transformative capacity.

THE LIMITS OF CASTORIADIS'S THINKING

We have been arguing that the thinker must ultimately respond to the challenge of history's apparent verdict—the claim that the project of autonomy is unrealisable—in so far as he, himself, is a politically committed bearer of this project and is therefore implicated in the project's retreat. Now we want to argue that it is precisely at this point, where Castoriadis acknowledges the gravity of the retreat from the standpoint of the thinker qua political activist, that his thinking falls short of the demands of the scope of the fundamental question for thinking. Firstly, the thinker of the project of autonomy who enacts its thinkability and, hence, demonstrates the justifiedness of its possibility, cannot simply refer descriptively to the political retreat of autonomy independently and prior to any acknowledgement of the need for a philosophical explanation of the empirical phenomenon. For this would be to reduce the difference between the thinker who affirms the possibility of autonomy and the one who rejects this possibility to two different interpretations of one and the same phenomenon—the fact of the project's historical failure—rather than to insist, as Castoriadis does, on a crucial difference between them in terms of the genuine place/fictive non-place distinction that he makes. Secondly, because Castoriadis takes his thinking to be integral to the project of autonomy in that it is itself an *autonomous thinking*, the project must be able to supply the justification for such thinking, and, at the same time, such thinking must be able to affirm the possibility of the political project. In other words, these two aspects must be mutually inform-ing. The combination of Castoriadis's philosophical ap-proach and his political commitment—the commitment to the autonomous collective as the proper subject matter of thinking—must make it possible for him to acknowledge the full scope of the question of thinking and, for present purposes, to specify the 'when and 'where' aspects of this question. Within Castoriadis's discourse that the thinking of autonomy is non-fictive in the sense that it has a genuine place must mean that its appropriate place within the project of autonomy is the very place within which the thinker en-counters the pure possibility of its thinkabiltiy. This is why Castoriadis cannot just declare the justifiedness of the proj-ect; just as politically he must position himself to practice autonomy effectively, so too qua thinker he must do position himself to act thinkingly. The very meaning of thinking au-tonomously is at issue here.

Indeed the appropriate response to the 'where' question holds that awareness of the political retreat must be trans-formed into a *philosophical* retreat and this can be achieved when the retreat of the collective happens *in the thinker*, so to speak. That is, the thinker must make the retreat happen in themselves as the thinking of the autonomous collective. This is the only way to make the thinking in question, the collective, which is the retreating gathering in the sense we have explained. We might say that in order to raise the ques-tion of the possibility of the autonomous collective as such, the gathering must retreat *in its retreat*. This is a second level of retreat that is itself implied by Castoriadis's acknowledge-ment of the retreat of the project of autonomy, the first level of retreat that he identifies in the failed political programs together with the absence of visible viable alternatives. Let us explain.

First, having retreated through the failure of specific po-litical programs the autonomous collective must be liber-ated from being identified with such particular manifesta-tions and the associated defeats. This is necessary precisely because the historical and theoretical verdict of the impossibility of autonomy implicates autonomy as such and not merely the specific failed programs. Second, because the thinker is called upon to affirm the justifiedness of the possibility of autonomy as such it will not suffice to challenge the verdict of history by elaborating another political program for the advancement of autonomy. To address the issue of whether the impossibility of autonomy can be justified theoretically, and not just as an inferred conclusion from the specific historical defeats of political programs, calls for a consideration of whether those failures are not the result of the impossibility of the project itself. But in such a case it is the project of autonomy as such that must be disassociated from its particular historical manifestations.

Now given that the experience of the project of autonomy is situated in the project's retreat via its association with the failed programs and awareness of the absence of viable alternatives, to thinkingly retrieve the project as such is to acknowledge the operation of what we referred to above as the 'second level of retreat', namely that from any and all specific programs. That is, in order to fully open himself to the challenge of the categorical verdict of history, Castoriadis must retrieve from history that which history has already brought forth, namely the question of the impossibility of autonomy as such as something over and above the specific/failed political programs. The only place available to the thinker in which to pursue the encounter of autonomy as such is the *topos* of retreat. This then is the place that the thinker must radicalize if the project of autonomy is to be resituated beyond the heteronomous spaces associated with the verdict of history.

If the above analysis is correct then it would appear that in order to recapture the project of autonomy philosophically, or, in its own pure possibility, the only option for the committed thinker is to make the project of autonomy retreat from the very spaces of the first retreat. From this perspective, to be a thinker is to treat one's thinking as the activity of the autonomous collective, which, in its retreating from the retreat of the political project, gathers itself in its own thinking activity and in doing so gives rise to its own historical possibility, albeit as visionary. So it is by facing the challenge of enacting this second level of retreat that the thinker enacts their autonomy qua thinker or, in other words, they become the thinker of the autonomous collective. Now, if the first retreat leads to the unwilling dispersion of the gathered members of the visionary collective, to the breaking down of this historical intervention of the significant collective, the second retreat can only take place willingly in the singular being of the thinker, giving rise to the thinker as gatherer who thinks/gathers the collective in its retreat. Such an act of thinking would involve gathering the significant aloneness of the collective through the cosmic void in the entirety of its past, present and future. Anything less would not amount to moving beyond the options available to proprietary being as regards thinking.[191]

Then if, as Castoriadis appears to acknowledge, the political possibilities for the re-activation of the project of autonomy are currently non-existent, in seeking thinkingly to affirm the possibility of re-activating the project of autonomy, the thinker must hold together, so to speak, *the visionary gathering in its retreat*. For it is this sort of radicalization of the retreat of the project that immanently disengages the investigation of the pure possibility of autonomy from that of the available political possibilities for the project's resurgence. Within such a framework, the very retreating of the autonomous collective is itself lost from view. After all, in attempting to engage the very *retreatingness* of the autonomous collective, for the reasons explained above, the thinker cannot simply identify this aspect of the gathering with the weaknesses of the failed programs. Nor, however, can he identify the collective's retreatingness with anything like

---

191. In our manuscript in progress, *1789 Philosphy: A-voiding Death in Modern Western Thought*, we explore the philosophical character of thinking in the gathering's retreat and argue that the limitations we have ascribed here to Castoriadis' thinking is a broader problem, which radical thinkers from Marx and Nietzsche, to Badiou and Deleuze have not succeeded in overcoming.

the thinker's anticipation qua activist of meaningful future opportunities for the resurgence of the political project. For, to do so would be to render meaningless the task of thinking the project's reactivation. It is only through the thinker's self-transformation into such a place of thinking the autonomous collective in its retreatedness that the thinker might hope to enact the possibility of the autonomous collective or, in other words, to justifiably reject the claim that the project of autonomy has been historically eliminated.

CONCLUSION

In the light of the above analysis and despite his best efforts, Castoriadis's recognition of the retreat of the project of autonomy appears as a merely journalistic intervention of the kind that he objects to, rather than as critique in the mode that he advocates. By limiting himself to what we identified above as the first level of retreat of the political project of autonomy, Castoriadis confines himself to the perspective of 'the creeping snake' and thus gives up the opportunity to engage with the project as the project of thinking. He merely reports on the rather obvious fact, that of the project's political retreat, without however relating to this retreat as the place of dwelling of the thinker, that is, as the genuine non--fictive place of the autonomous collective and thus as the *topos* in which the autonomous gathering might be retrievable from the spaces of its historical rejection.

7. IN PLACE OF A CONCLUSION

Having concluded that Castoriadis's mode of thinking ultimately falls short of the demands raised for it by the retreat
of the project of autonomy, we end this study with a return
to the idea of the artist as gatherer, which we introduced at
the outset with our brief discussion of David's *The Tennis
Court Oath*. Like David, in his painting *The Third of May 1808*
Francesco de Goya depicts a scene that calls our attention to
the gathering but in the case of Goya's painting, the scene—
the execution of Spanish patriots by the occupying French
army—manifests a tragic moment of retreat of the French
Revolutionary collective and its radical aspirations. That is, in
moving from *The Tennis Court Oath* to *The Third of May* we
move from an artistic expression of irruption of the communal gathering to that of its retreat. In contrast to *The Tennis
Court Oath*, *The Third of May* portrays the human gathering
as the abyss of an infinite self-cancelling in the sense of a can-
celling of the communal gathering's visionary agency. This
cancelled agency takes place on two levels. On one level, the
schism of death, which is visually produced with the aid of
the line of faceless victims moving towards those who have
already fallen, that is, the space of death that Goya's lantern illuminates, represents the moment of retreat from the visionary gathering. The space of death forms a schism between the
indeterminate communal gathering, depicted as the mass of
victims, and the formed gathering, the firing squad, which
remains uninformed by communality. The schism is flood-
ed by the void of cosmic indifference. On a second level, as

signified by the centred figure of the martyr, the self is also a site of the schism, namely that between the singular being of the individual and its communal singularity. In this sense, in stark contrast to the central figure of *The Tennis Court Oath* gatherer, Goya's martyr enacts the being of the gatherer as a participant in the cancelled gathering. Given these new experiences of the gathering, whether as visionary or as a dystopian self-annihilation, the gathering is enacted through participants' singular being in their dual capacity as gathered and as gatherers. For the artist this enactment of the cancelled gathering is just as disturbing as the loss of lives through which it is visually portrayed.

The abovementioned dual association of the gathering with the schism of death has Goya desperately seeking to close the gap between the formless and formed aspects of the gathering of death or, in other words, to overcome the time of death itself. This desperation is revealed through the movement that *The Third of May* produces from the face of the martyr to the firing squad and back. The light of the lantern illuminates the scene of *The Third of May* so as to initially focus the viewer's attention on the despairing face of the martyr who faces the firing squad with upraised arms. This is the visual starting point for the viewer. Unlike the face of David's gatherer, the face of the martyr holds vision *and death* together as the focal point of the catastrophe. The visual field then unfolds as the viewer moves across the landscape of death to arrive at the site of the firing squad. On completion of this movement from the face of the martyr through the crossing of the schism to the soldiers, this path is then traversed in the reverse direction. The eye of the viewer, which follows the line created by the firearms, also moves towards the face of the martyr crossing the schism from the position of the firing squad. The disproportionality of the distance between the formless and formed aspects of the gathering ensures this two-directional movement, thus manifesting the artist's longing to close the unbridgeable gap. Accompanying this longing, however, is a suggestion of ambivalence concerning the world of the schism.

The ambivalence in question is suggested by Goya's initial self-positioning beyond the illuminated site of the schism. With the abovementioned movement from the martyr to the soldiers, the artist's ambivalence becomes apparent with the observation that he has positioned himself (and the viewer), not on the side of the martyr but directly behind the firing squad. Even though the artist/viewer does not identify with the firing squad, in being positioned behind the soldiers one is nonetheless implicated in this technological world of violence, the world that is already constituted by the schism that the retreat has opened up. This is the world Goya produces artistically with the centring of the famous lantern. The combination of Goya's ambivalence towards an emerging technological world and his longing to overcome the schism reveal the powerlessness of the artist in this context.

Nonetheless, in being embedded in the world of the schism the viewer participates through their singular being without, however, being absorbed in the gathering's violent form. Unlike the firing squad, the viewer is positioned to recognize in the face of the martyr the gathering's visionary singularity. This is to embody the schism of death, which is at once the schism between singular being and communal singularity. Goya's viewer must therefore dwell in the time of death while pointing to the cancelled gathering, the retreated singularity that occupies the other side of the schism in the centred figure of the martyr. Although in visually opening the schism of death Goya ultimately places both himself and the viewer in the time of death, he is not also in a position to question the meaning of death and challenge its origins. This latter we suggest is a task for the philosopher who manages to move beyond the limits of Castoriadian thinking as identified in this study. Dwelling in the time and place of the retreat of the project of autonomy calls upon the philosopher to thinkingly hold together vision and death.

REFERENCES

Adams, Suzi, 'Interpreting Creation: Castoriadis and the Birth of Autonomy', *Thesis Eleven*, vol. 83, 2005, pp. 25-41.

Adams, Suzi, *Castoriadis's Ontology: Being and Creation*, New York, Fordham University Press, 2011.

Badiou, Alain, 'The Democratic Emblem' in Giorgio Agamben, Alain Badiou, Daniel Bensaid, Wendy Brown, Jean-Luc Nancy, Jacques Rancière, Kristin Ross, and Slavoj Žižek, trans. William McCuaig, *Democracy in What State?* New York, Columbia University Press, 2012, pp. 6-15.

Baruchello, Giorgio, 'Old Bedfellows: Cornelius Castoriadis on Capitalism and Freedom', in Ingrid S. Straume and Giorgio Baruchello (eds.), *Creation Rationality and Autonomy: Essays on Cornelius Castoriadis*, Copenhagen, Denmark, Aarhus University Press NSU, 2013, pp. 101-129.

Brown, Wendy, 'We are all Democrats Now ...' in Giorgio Agamben, Alain Badiou, Daniel Bensaid, Wendy Brown, Jean-Luc Nancy, Jacques Rancière, Kristin Ross, and Slavoj Žižek, trans. William McCuaig, *Democracy in What State?* New York, Columbia University Press, 2012, pp. 44-57.

Castoriadis, Cornelius, *Crossroads in the Labyrinth*, Sussex, Harvester Press, 1984.

Castoriadis, Cornelius, *The Imaginary Institution of Society*, Cambridge, Polity Press, 1987.

Castoriadis, Cornelius, *Political and Social Writings, Vol. I 1946-55*, Minneapolis, University of Minnesota Press, 1988.

Castoriadis, Cornelius, *Philosophy Politics Autonomy: Essays in Political Philosophy*, New York, Oxford, Oxford University Press, 1991.

Castoriadis, Cornelius, 'The Dilapidation of the West', *Thesis Eleven*, vol. 41, no. 1, 1995, pp. 94-111.

Castoriadis, Cornelius, 'The Greek Πόλις and the Creation of Democracy' in R. Lily, (ed.), *The Ancients and the Moderns*, Bloomington, Indiana, Indiana University Press, 1996, pp. 29-58.

Castoriadis, Cornelius, 'Democracy as Procedure and Democracy as Regime' *Constellations*, vol. 4, no. 1, 1997, pp. 1-18.

Castoriadis, Cornelius, *The Castoriadis Reader*, in David Ames Curtis (ed), Oxford, UK, Blackwell Publishers, 1997.

Castoriadis, Cornelius, *World in Fragments: Writings on Politics, Society, Psychoanalysis and the Imagination*. California, Stanford University Press, 1997.

Castoriadis, Cornelius, *On Plato's Statesman*, Stanford, CA, Stanford University Press, 2002.

Castoriadis, Cornelius, *Figures of the Thinkable*, trans. Helen Arnold, Stanford, CA, Stanford University Press, 2007.

Castoriadis, Cornelius, *Postscript on Insignificance*, trans. G Rockhill and J V Garner, New York, Continuum, 2011.

Ciaramelli, Fabio, 'The Self-presupposition of the Origin: Homage to Cornelius Castoriadis', *Thesis Eleven*, no. 49, 1997, pp. 45-67.

Davis, David, O, *A Theology of Compassion*, Michigan, Cambridge, Eerdmans, 2003.

Egumenovska, Kristina, 'The Wreath of Subjectivity and Time', in Ingrid S. Straume and Giorgio Baruchello (eds.), *Creation Rationality and Autonomy: Essays on Cornelius Castoriadis*, Copenhagen, Denmark, Aarhus University Press NSU, 2013, pp. 229-241.

Elliott, Anthony, 'New Individualist Configurations and the

Social Imaginary: Castoriadis and Kristeva', *European Journal of Social Theory*, vol. 15, no. 3, 2012, pp. 349- 365.

Fotopoulos, Takis, 'The Autonomy Project and Inclusive Democracy: A Critical Review of Castoriadis' Thought', *The International Journal of Inclusive Democracy*, vol. 4, no. 2. 2008, pp. 1-13.

Fraser, Nancy, 'Rethinking the Public Sphere' in Simon During (ed.), *The Cultural Studies Reader*, London and New York, Routledge, Second edition, 1993, pp. 516-536.

Gourgouris, Stathis, 'Autonomy and Self-alteration', in Ingrid S. Straume and Giorgio Baruchello (eds.), *Creation Rationality and Autonomy: Essays on Cornelius Castoriadis*, Copenhagen, Denmark, Aarhus University Press NSU, 2013, pp. 243-268.

Heap, Jodi, *The Imagination: The Seed of Indeterminacy in the Writings of Kant, Fichte and Castoriadis*, PhD dissertation, University of Melbourne, 2017.

Hegel, G. W. F., *The Phenomenology of Spirit*, Oxford, Oxford University Press, 1970.

Hegel, G. W. F., *Philosophy of Right*, trans. T M Knox, Oxford, Oxford University Press, 1981.

Hegel, G. W. F., *Philosophy of History*, trans. J Sibree, New York, Dover Publications, 1956.

Heller, Agnes, 'Philosophy as Literary Genre', *Thesis Eleven*, vol. 10, no. 1, 2012, pp. 17-26.

Honneth, Axel, 'Rescuing the Revolution with an Ontology: On Cornelius Castoriadis' Theory of Society', *Thesis Eleven*, no. 14, 1986, pp. 62-78.

Kalyvas Andreas, 'The Radical Instituting Power and Democratic Theory' *Journal of the Hellenic Diaspora*, vol. 24, no. 1, 1998, pp. 9-28.

Kalyvas Andreas, 'The Politics of Autonomy and the Challenge of Deliberation: Castoriadis contra Habermas', *Thesis Eleven*, vol. 64, 2001, pp. 1–19.

Karagiannis, Natalie, 'The Tragic and the Political: A Parallel Reading of Kostas Papaioannou and Cornelius Castoriadis', *Critical Horizons*, vol. 7, no. 1, 2006, pp. 303-319.

Karagiannis, Natalie and Wagner, Peter, 'What Is to Be Thought? What Is to Be Done? The Polyscopic Thought of Kostas Axelos and Cornelius Castoriadis', *European Journal of Social Theory*, vol. 15, no. 3, 2012, pp. 403-417.

Karalis, Vrasidas, 'Introduction to Cornelius Castoriadis's Early Essays', in *Cornelius Castoriadis and Radical Democracy*, Vrasidas Karalis (ed.), Leiden and Boston, Brill, 2014, pp. 1-20.

Karavitis, Gerasimos, 'On the Concept of Politics: A Comparative Reading of Castoriadis and Badiou', *Constellations*, vol. 25, 2018, pp. 256-271.

Kioupkiolis, Alexandros, 'The Agonistic Turn of Critical Reason: Critique and Freedom in Foucault and Castoriadis', *European Journal of Social Theory*, vol. 15, no. 3, 2012, pp. 385-402.

Klimis, Sophie 'From Modernity to Neoliberalism: What Human Subject?', in Ingrid S. Straume and Giorgio Baruchello (eds.), *Creation Rationality and Autonomy: Essays on Cornelius Castoriadis*, Copenhagen, Denmark, Aarhus University Press NSU, 2013, pp. 133-158.

Klooger, Jeff, 'From Nothing: Castoriadis and the Concept of Creation', *Critical Horizons*, vol. 12, no.1, 2011, pp. 29-47.

Klooger, Jeff, 'Plurality and Indeterminacy: Revisiting Castoriadis's overly Homogeneous Conception of Society', *European Journal of Social Theory*, 2011, pp. 1-17.

Klooger, Jeff, 'The Guise of Nothing: Castoriadis on Indeterminacy, and its Misrecognition in Heidegger and Sartre', *Critical Horizons* vol. 14, no. 1, 2013, pp. 1-21.

Klooger, Jeff, *Castoriadis: Psyche, Society, Autonomy*, Leiden and Boston, Brill, 2009.

Labelle, Gilles, 'Two Refoundation Projects of Democracy in Contemporary French Philosophy: Cornelius Castoriadis and Jacques Rancière', *Philosophy and Social Criticism*, vol. 27, no. 4. 2001, pp. 75-103.

Mouzakitis, Angelos, 'Chaos and Creation in Castoriadis's

Interpretation of Greek Thought', in Ingrid S. Straume and Giorgio Baruchello (eds.), *Creation Rationality and Autonomy: Essays on Cornelius Castoriadis*, Copenhagen, Denmark, Aarhus University Press, 2013, NSU, pp. 31-48.

Nicolacopoulos, Toula and Vassilacopoulos, George, 'The Pulse of Chronos: Historical Time, the Eternal and Timelessness in the Platonic Gathering', *Parrhesia*, vol. 15, 2012, pp. 54-63.

Nicolacopoulos, Toula and Vassilacopoulos, George, *Hegel and the Logical Structure of Love: An Essay on Sexualities, Families and the Law*, Melbourne, re.press, 2010.

Nicolacopoulos, Toula and Vassilacopoulos, George, *The Disjunctive Logic Of The World: Thinking Global Civil Society With Hegel*, Melbourne, re.press, 2013.

Nicolacopoulos, Toula, *The Radical Critique of Liberalism*, Seddon, re.press, 2008.

Oikonomou, Yorgos, 'Plato and Castoriadis: The Concealment and the Unravelling of Democracy', *The International Journal of Inclusive Democracy*, vol. 2, no. 1. 2005, pp. 1-15.

Ojeili, Chamsy, 'Post-Marxism with Substance', *New Political Science*, vol. 23, no. 2, 2001, pp. 225-239

Papadimitropoulos, Vangelis, 'Indeterminacy and creation in the work of Cornelius Castoriadis', *Cosmos and History: Journal of Natural and Social Philosophy*, vol. 11, no. 1, 2015, pp. 256-268.

Papadimitropoulos, Vangelis, 'Rational Mastery in the Work of Cornelius Castoriadis', *Capitalism Nature Socialism*, vol. 29, no. 3, 2018.

Plato, *The Republic*, Penguin, 1987.

Premat, Chirstophe, 'Castoriadis and the Modern Political Imaginary—Oligarchy, Representation, Democracy', *Critical Horizons*, vol. 7, no. 1., pp. 251-275.

Rawls, John, *Political Liberalism*, Columbia University Press, 1993.

Rundell, John, 'Autonomy, Oligarchy, Statesman: Weber, Castoriadis and the Fragility of Politics', in Vrasidas

Karalis, (ed.), *Cornelius Castoriadis and Radical Democracy*, Leiden and Boston: Brill, 2014, pp. 262-290.

Smith, Karl E, *Meaning Subjectivity Society: Making Sense of Modernity*, Leiden and Boston, Brill, 2010.

Smith, Karl, E, 'The Constitution of Modernity: A Critique of Castoriadis', *European Journal of Social Theory*, vol. 12, no. 4, pp. 505-521.

Straume, Ingrid S, 'A Common World: Arendt Castoriadis and Political Creation', *European Journal of Social Theory*, vol. 15, no. 3, 2012, pp. 367-383.

Straume, Ingrid S, 'Castoriadis, Education and Democracy', in Ingrid S. Straume and Giorgio Baruchello (eds.), *Creation Rationality and Autonomy: Essays on Cornelius Castoriadis*, Copenhagen, Denmark, Aarhus University Press NSU, 2013, pp. 203-228.

Vouldis, Angelos, T, 'Cornelius Castoriadis on the Scope and Content of Neoclassical and Marxian Economics', *Journal of Economic Issues*, vol. 52, no. 3, 2018.

Watson, Irene, 'First Nations, Indigenous Peoples: Our Laws Have Always Been Here', in Irene Watson (ed.) *Indigenous Peoples as Subjects of International Law*, Routledge, EBook Central, 2017.

Whitebook, Joel, 'Intersubjectivity and the Monadic Core of the Psyche: Habermas and Castoriadis on the Unconscious', *Praxis International*, no. 4, 1989, pp. 347-364.

Whitebook, Joel, 'Review of Crossroads in the Labyrinth', *Telos*, vol. 63, 1985, p. 23.

Wolf, Harald, 'The Power of the Imaginary', in Ingrid S. Straume and Giorgio Baruchello (eds.), *Creation Rationality and Autonomy: Essays on Cornelius Castoriadis*, Copenhagen, Denmark, Aarhus University Press NSU, 2013, pp. 185-201.

Zerilli, Linda MG,'Castoriadis Arendt and the Problem of the New', *Constellations*, vol. 9, no. 2., 2002, pp. 540-553.

* 9 7 8 0 9 9 2 3 7 3 4 5 0 *